Ideology and Power
in Soviet Politics

IDEOLOGY
AND
POWER
IN
SOVIET POLITICS

Zbigniew K. Brzezinski

GREENWOOD PRESS, PUBLISHERS
WESTPORT, CONNECTICUT

Library of Congress Cataloging in Publication Data

Brzezinski, Zbigniew K   1928-
  Ideology and power in Soviet politics.

    Reprint of the ed. published by Praeger, New York,
which was issued as no. 103 of Praeger publications in
Russian history and world communism.
  Includes bibliographies.
    1. Russia--Politics and government--1917-
2. Communism--History. I. Title.
[JN6515 1962.B7 1976]   320.9'47'085   76-6571
ISBN 0-8371-8880-6

© 1962 by Frederick A. Praeger, Inc.

Originally published in 1962 by Frederick A. Praeger,
Publishers, New York

Reprinted with the permission of Praeger Publishers, Inc.

Reprinted in 1976 by Greenwood Press, Inc.,
51 Riverside Avenue, Westport, Conn. 06880

Library of Congress catalog card number 76-6571
ISBN 0-8371-8880-6

Printed in the United States of America

10 9 8 7 6 5 4 3

Contents

Part II
FOREIGN AFFAIRS

Ideology and Power
in Soviet Politics

Introduction

The purpose of this short volume is not to convince but, hopefully, to stimulate. Each of the five essays argues a thesis of its own, about either domestic or international Soviet politics. The first essay is a discussion of the general character of totalitarianism and its relationship to a modern, "rationally" operated industrial society; the second a consideration of the problems of continuity and change between the Czarist and Soviet political executives; and the third an analysis of the nature of the contemporary Soviet political system. The remaining two essays are devoted to international aspects: an examination of the role of ideology in the Soviet world outlook, with special attention to the prospects of ideological relativization and erosion; and an assessment of the changes that have taken place in the political and ideological relations prevailing among the Communist states.

The close interaction of ideology and power in both internal and external Communist politics is the theme that links the essays together. The distinction between ideological and power considerations, often made when Soviet conduct is analyzed, appears to this author to be,

3

first of all, an artificial abstraction and, secondly, a rather misleading issue. Soviet political leaders, being politicians, naturally are preoccupied with the maintenance of power and with its maximization. But political power in every circumstance involves purpose, assessment, communication, action, and legitimization. It is impossible to wield power, to exercise it effectively, and especially to use it actively unless there is a sharing of certain values, implicitly or overtly, among the leaders, the ruling elite, and (particularly in our age) the masses. This is particularly so in the case of a movement with a history of acute ideological ferment, somewhat like the intense religious debates of earlier times. There is a natural tendency in this movement to elevate major issues into matters of principle and to try to fit actions into a general framework. Furthermore, when the movement is built around an ideology that combines both an overt statement of normative ends and a set of intellectual categories for analyzing changes in the existing reality with specific guides to action, then considerations of ideology and power become so enmeshed in the performance of a particular political act that to isolate one from the other is to deny that which is precisely most characteristic of the movement—the blending of ideology with power.

Although it is dangerous to attempt to reduce the meaning of ideology to a one-sentence statement, the following might be suggested as merely a working definition: It is essentially an action program suitable for mass consumption, derived from certain doctrinal assumptions about the general nature of the dynamics of social reality, and combining some assertions about the inadequacies of the past

4

and/or present with some explicit guides to action for improving the situation and some notions of the desired eventual state of affairs. Ideology thus combines action—and since its object is society, it must be political action—with a consciousness both of purpose and of the general thrust of history. It gives its adherents a sense of consistency and certainty that is too often absent among those who have been brought up in the tradition of short-range pragmatism and empiricism. Commitment to the ideology establishes a standard for discriminating between the important and the unimportant. It encourages the ideologically oriented politician to engage in programmatic thinking, to ask himself repeatedly these questions: What is the real meaning of my historical epoch? What are the motor forces changing reality in our lifetime? How can I best relate myself to those changes so that both my power and my ends are well served?

Few Western statesmen do this. Some, like De Gaulle, do because of their personal, instinctive sense of history. But most, especially those who operate in the Anglo-Saxon tradition, usually do not—reflecting the spontaneous and organic development of their societies, which for many decades have not had to pause and examine consciously their social organization, their purposes, their direction. Their policies naturally tend to be both more pragmatic and more reactive than those of ideologically oriented leaders. But it does not follow, as often assumed, that the nonideological Western leaders are therefore more "rational" than the Communists. The matter of political rationality depends very much on the actual content of the ideology itself. The Nazi leaders, for instance, adhered to an ideology that so obscured their vision as to make them repeatedly engage in actions that were irrational even in terms of their own purposes. The Communist leaders, however, subscribe to an ideology that, whatever the rationality of their ultimate ends and basic assumptions may be, has given them some insight into the contemporary anticolonial and industrial revolutions. While, as some of the essays show, it has often led them into dogmatic stands, their ideology has also given them a keen appreciation of contemporary social and political dynamics, an appreciation often lacking among their *dogmatically* undogmatic Western opponents.

Indeed, one could even argue that the Communist ideology involves such a conscious emphasis on the development of skillful political strategies and tactics, and on always relating the latter to the former, that the chances of "irrational" conduct on the part of the Communists are not greater than those of their more pragmatic Western opponents (particularly Anglo-Saxon ones). For example, Suez in 1956 and Cuba in 1961 provide good illustrations of desperation and impatience leading us into what might be appropriately described as irrational conduct. In both cases, the chief Western errors were failures of theoretical and ideological omission, and from them followed the military and logistical inadequacies. The theoretical error involved the failure to perceive that in Nasser and in Castro one was dealing no longer with a traditional-type system that could be overthrown from within by the application of merely limited external force. Both leaders have successfully eliminated intermediary social groups and skillfully mobilized the masses.

6

Introduction

What is the political nature of our opponent? That question was either not raised or inadequately answered. Ideologically, both cases involved failures to assess the long-range and more basic forces at work—in one the intensifying wave of awakened Arab nationalism, in the other a left-wing revolution that could only be effectively countered through the mobilization of the democratic left rather than of the center and the right. In both, the "case method" and the common-law tradition of viewing each issue in isolation resulted in the loss of the broader perspective and led to actions that history may judge disdainfully.

The Communists, however, have frequently tended to the other extreme—namely toward the elevation of their social, economic, and political system of analysis into a semireligious, absolute dogma. The reason for this lies primarily in their political history: in the linkage of the ideology with a one-party dictatorship, usually led by a personal dictator. This condition eliminated creative dialogue and disagreement. It equated the decision of the dictator with infallible ideological insight. And it has often resulted in grievous errors. Perhaps the somewhat more diversified situation prevailing today in the Communist bloc (see Chapter 5) may lead to more regular discussions within the Communist movement, and thus gradually overcome the inherent tendency toward dogmatism and arrogant self-righteousness so characteristic of contemporary Communism. However, this would eventually require a major change in the nature of the movement itself (see Chapters 3 and 4).

At the same time, the challenge posed by the Communists might force the West to examine more consciously and more purposefully the meaning and the direction of the flow of history, to try to relate the past to the present and to seek in that relationship some clearer and longer-range insights into the future—and perhaps even to subordinate our interests of today to the imperatives of tomorrow. The Western tradition of open and creative debate could fortify our statesmen, since it presents them with a less dogmatic basis for engaging in programmatic thinking of the sort that has long been overdue.

The issues raised in this introduction are the outgrowth of the essays. They certainly need much more elaboration and thought. Perhaps some readers will be provoked into doing just that. If they are, the republication of these essays, which have previously appeared separately, will have been justified.

"Totalitarianism and Rationality" was first published in *The American Political Science Review* (September, 1956). "Patterns of Autocracy" appeared as a chapter in a collective volume edited by C. E. Black, *The Transformation in Russian Society* (Cambridge, Mass.: Harvard University Press, 1960). "The Nature of the Soviet System" appeared in *Slavic Review* (October, 1961). "Communist Ideology and International Affairs" is reprinted from the *Journal of Conflict Resolution* (September, 1960). "The Challenge of Change in the Soviet Bloc" first appeared in *Foreign Affairs* (April, 1961; copyright © 1961 by the Council on Foreign Relations, Inc., New York). To the editors and publishers of the above go my thanks for allowing the essays to be collected in this vol-

Introduction

ume. For purposes of consistency and to take into account recent events, a number of minor editorial changes have been made and some repetitions eliminated. I am also grateful to The Russian Institute of Columbia University for its support.

ZBIGNIEW BRZEZINSKI

July, 1961
Englewood, N.J.

Part I

INTERNAL POLITICS

1. Totalitarianism and Rationality

The experience of modern totalitarian regimes suggests that they are not likely to perish through internal revolt unless it occurs at a time when the totalitarian regime is in mortal danger from an external challenge, as in the marginal Italian case, or when the totalitarian movement in power is about to undertake decisive measures to turn the country into a totalitarian system, as in the case of the counterrevolution against Perón in Argentina. Other than that, and even considering the succession crises, modern totalitarian regimes have shown themselves capable of maintaining their totalitarian character in spite of domestic and foreign opposition. More recently, it has been argued (e.g., by Deutscher, in *Russia: What Next?*) that modern totalitarian regimes, if not overthrown by external forces, nevertheless in the end will be quietly and inevitably transformed into more democratic states by the subtler but irresistible influence of rationality inherent in the bureaucratic and managerial apparatus that no modern state can do without. This proposition will be developed more fully and given critical consideration in subsequent pages in order to test whether rationality, regarded in this context as a certain mode of thought and behavior induced by the requirements of modern industrialized and bureaucratized societies, is in fact incompatible with modern totalitarianism. To do this, however, we first have to seek some specific political definition of the system of rule currently known as "totalitarianism." A preliminary attempt to posit a working definition and to discuss the process of totalitarian development in terms that might justify the application of the term "totalitarian" to such otherwise varied systems as the Nazi, the Soviet, and possibly the fascist ones thus seems proper.

A Definition of Totalitarianism

The crux of any attempted definition of totalitarianism is the perplexing issue of its uniqueness: What is distinctively new about it? Certainly, autocratic systems in the past displayed many of the features developed and accentuated by modern totalitarianism. Diocletian's tyranny or the Shogunate in Japan, for instance, stressed to a high degree the acquiescence of the population in centralized control. Both systems also institutionalized an atmosphere of fear through a system of secret-police informers not unlike the totalitarian societies of the twentieth century. Similarly, we find among many of the nineteenth-century European reformers a readiness to use violence for the sake of postulated improvements and reforms much like the ideological intolerance and consequent brutality of the Rosenbergs or Zhdanovs of our own age.[1] Cromwell's regime also displayed some analogies. The examples could easily be multiplied to include many other cases involving features similar to some of the characteristics of totalitarianism. Spain is a contemporary example.

Totalitarianism, being a dictatorship, characteristically includes the coercive qualities noted in such varied dictatorial systems. But unlike most dictatorships of the past and present, the totalitarian movements wielding power do not aim to freeze society in the status quo; on the contrary, their aim is to institutionalize a revolution that mounts in scope, and frequently in intensity, as the regime stabilizes itself in power. The purpose of this revolution is to pulverize all existing social units in order to replace the old pluralism with a homogeneous unanimity patterned on the blueprints of the totalitarian ideology. The power of the totalitarian regime is derived not from a precarious balance of existing forces (e.g., church, landed gentry, officer corps), but from the revolutionary dynamism of its zealous supporters, who disarm opposition and mobilize the masses both by force and by an appeal to a better future. This appeal is normally framed in the official ideology, or action program, of the movement. In time, of course, the dynamism decreases, but by then the system is buttressed by complex networks of control that pervade the entire society and mobilize its energies through sheer penetration. An institutionalized revolution, patterned on the totalitarian ideology, thus makes totalitarianism essentially a forward-oriented phenomenon. Most dictatorships, on the other hand, have as their object the prevention of history from keeping in step with time. Their survival depends on maintaining the status quo. When they fail, they become history.*

This proposition can be further developed by examining the fate of restraints on political power—which are present in varying degrees in all societies, once the totalitarian movement seizes power. These restraints can be broadly listed in three categories: 1) the direct restraints, expressed through *pacta conventa* such as the English Magna Charta or the Polish *Nihil novi* . . . , the Bill of Rights, constitutional guarantees, a rule of law, or even the broad consensus of tradition that rules out certain types of conduct, such as the use of violence; 2) the indirect restraints that stem from the pluralistic character of all large-scale societies, necessitating adjustment and compromise as the basis for political power—e.g., the churches, the economic interests, professional, cultural, or regional pressure groups, all of which impede the exercise of unrestrained power; and 3) the natural restraints, such as national character and tradition, climatic and geographical considerations, kinship structure, and particularly the primary social unit, the family. These also act to restrain the scope of political power.†

In constitutional societies, all three categories of re-

---

* This is the political tragedy of such leaders as Chiang Kai-shek and Nagib, who came to power to effect a revolution, but became dependent in their control of power on conservative elements.

† One might also consider a supernatural restraint in the sense of a transcendent moral order to which many governments pay lip service. In fact, however, its *political* significance is probably covered fully by the three outlined above, and particularly by the first two.

straint are operative on political power. In practice, of course, various violations occur, but these generally constitute a deviation from the norm rather than the norm itself. Dictatorial or ancient autocratic societies are characterized by the absence of the direct restraints, since these are incompatible with the nature of arbitrary, and frequently personal, leadership. Suspension of civil rights, open or masked subversion of established constitutional practices, and negation of popular sovereignty have been characteristic of all nonconstitutional states, whether totalitarian or not.

The indirect restraints, however, have usually escaped the dictatorial scythe except when a significant social grouping chooses to resist directly the dictates of those in power. If, for instance, the church or the nobility, for one reason or another, clashes with the ruler, it is then subjected to the dictatorial pattern of coercion. Generally, however, the broad outlines of social life are not disturbed by the dictator even though an individual objector, even in a high place, is struck down. An average Hungarian under Horthy or a Frenchman under Louis XIV was not directly drawn into the operations of the regime and could continue in his traditional associations much as before the advent of the ruler. The ruler himself based his power to a great extent on the varying alliances reached among combinations of social-political forces and maintained himself in power as long as such alliances endured. Revolutionary changes were hence anathema to a dictatorship of this kind.

It is only totalitarianism of our own age that rejects all

17

three kinds of restraints.* It not only subverts the direct restraints immediately after the seizure of power but, unlike traditional dictatorships, it proceeds, once entrenched, to destroy all existing associations in society in order to remake that society and, subsequently, even man himself, according to certain "ideal" conceptions. In time, it even attempts, not always successfully, to overcome the natural restraints on political power. Without doing so, totalitarianism can never achieve the isolation of the individual and the mass monolithic homogeneity that are its aim. Only with both of them (the paradox between them is more apparent than real) can the existing pluralism be changed to an active unanimity of the entire population that will make the transformation of society, and ultimately of man, possible. Only through them can man be conditioned to the totalitarian image, for the totalitarian hope is that action patterns will lead to thought patterns. This process, however, even if purposely gradual (as, for instance, in Poland under the Communists), inevitably involves the regime in increasing applications of coercion. Some of the "unredeemable social misfits" have to be removed, and it is difficult for the regime to single out for extinction particular social groups without soon involving itself in large-scale terror. Society is composed, after all, of largely overlapping associations and loyalties. Terror thus becomes an inevitable consequence, as well as instrument, of the revolutionary program. But the totalitarian revolution would be meaningless without a justi-

---

* Democracies do so, to a limited extent, in time of recognized danger; this is the concept of constitutional dictatorship. However, it always has some time limit.

18

fication to induce the active unanimity of the population. Hence, ideology is not merely a historical guide. It becomes a daily dose of perpetual indoctrination. The total social impact of the totalitarian efforts to make reality conform to totalitarian thought, involving terror and indoctrination as well as institutional and social reorganization, makes for a quantitative difference from old dictatorships that is sufficiently great to become a qualitative difference.

In order to define totalitarianism, one may also attempt to isolate its objective attributes, some of which have already been implied. Carl J. Friedrich suggests that these may include, in a syndrome, the following: an official ideology, a single mass party, a technologically conditioned near-complete monopoly of all means of effective armed combat and of effective mass communication, and a system of terroristic police control.[2] The combination of these by no means exclusively totalitarian characteristics with the total social impact stemming from the inherently dynamic revolutionary spirit of totalitarianism makes it, in terms of the accepted categorizations of political systems, historically distinct. Totalitarianism, therefore, has to be considered as a new form of government falling into the general classification of dictatorship, which includes the ancient autocracies, tyrannies, despotisms, absolute monarchies, and traditional dictatorships. Totalitarianism is a system in which technologically advanced instruments of political power are wielded without restraint by centralized leadership of an elite movement, for the purpose of effecting a total social revolution, including the conditioning of man, on the basis of certain arbitrary ideological assumptions proclaimed by the leadership, in an atmosphere of coerced unanimity of the entire population.[3] This definition thus goes beyond Friedrich's descriptive syndrome of discernible characteristics of totalitarianism and attempts to point also to its essence—i.e., its institutionalized revolutionary zeal.

DYNAMICS

Existing political situations in a number of countries provide useful illustrations of the stages of totalitarian development. Admittedly, these overlap. In France and Italy, the totalitarian movements operate today, competing electorally and plotting conspiratorially, in a non-totalitarian environment. Their task is to overthrow, at an opportune moment, the existing political systems and to seize power as a prerequisite to the implementation of their programmatic goals. Their situation, broadly speaking, is analogous to the position of the NSDAP in the Weimar Republic prior to 1933 or of the Bolsheviks in Russia prior to 1917, although the latter had to rely much more on conspiratorial action. This is the pre-revolutionary stage, which may range through varying phases of maturity and ripening before the actual moment of seizure of power.

The next stage follows the seizure of power, with the totalitarian movement solidifying its hold on the instruments of power. This is the period of entrenchment, of occasional compromise, of preparation. Active opposition elements are removed, and comprehensive plans for future operations drafted. Gradual efforts to penetrate and neutralize hitherto abstaining groups, which could become potential sources of resistance, are made in anticipation of their total absorption. This was the situation prevailing in Italy during almost the entire Fascist period,* in Germany roughly until the war, in the U.S.S.R. until the early 1930's, and in Argentina until the actual collapse of the Perónist regime when it was about to embark on its revolutionary program. It is thus a stage of consolidation and anticipation, of tactical appeasements masking strategic planning.

The totalitarian system begins to materialize with the launching of the internal revolution and the attempted destruction of existing social units. At this stage, not only the indirect restraints but even the so-called natural ones are assaulted. As the image and the structure of the totalitarian movement come to be reflected in the new institutions, organizations, and factories built on the ashes of the old society, the system takes shape. In all walks of life, the operational principles of the movement become the standards for conduct, and the race into the future starts. All the energies of the population are mobilized through force, rewards, opportunities, and propaganda. Ideology, reduced to the level of the daily exhortation, is used to justify the existing sacrifices and to give meaning to the unending search for the ideal tomorrow. This is the situation initiated in the U.S.S.R. by the First Five-Year Plan, and in the satellites since about 1948.

* Fascist inability to cope decisively with the old officer corps, the monarchy, and the Vatican probably also explains the relative swiftness of the collapse of Fascist power as compared with the Nazi capacity to control the situation until the final annihilation.

Inevitably, however, stabilizing factors begin to inter-
vene even before the full impetus of the internal revolution is felt. Power, like wealth, has an inherent tendency
to attract strong attachments in those who enjoy it. Consequently, the triumphant elite, while not officially abandoning its ultimate ends, tends to stress immediate power
considerations. An ideological rationalization for such a
tendency is ever ready: Power must be consolidated if
further advances are to be made. The sincerity or insin-
cerity of such reasoning notwithstanding, the consolidation of power becomes a conservative tendency. In an
ideologically motivated, zealous organization, this breeds
its own antithesis among those anxious to push ahead.
Those who toiled and risked to seize power accordingly
become all the more fearful of the rising young stars and
new constellations in the movement, into which many
late arrivals have flocked. Some therefore urge that revolutionary changes be pushed immediately lest new elements
come to the fore. Others urge greater restraint and even
compromise with the former dominant groups, now sup-
pressed but still not liquidated. Purges provide a partial
solution for this dissension. The history of the right- and
left-wing deviations in the U.S.S.R., and of the SA-SS
clash in Germany, is instructive in this respect. The intervention of such stabilizing factors, in the initial stages at
least, thus tends merely to accentuate the tension. Its
longer-run consequence, however, so far as available experience indicates, is to generate even greater violence and
unpredictability.

But in time, other pressures toward gradualism and
stability develop. As the ruling elite ages, it becomes

more and more concerned with succession, with status, and also with the transmission of its privileges to its children. Revolutionary considerations begin to be obscured by a desire to assure one's own offspring better education, advancement opportunities, etc. Such processes develop unconsciously as an inevitable consequence of privilege. Distinct class differentiation thus develops, producing another element impeding the totalitarian revolution, which tends to emphasize social mobility, arbitrariness, and uncertainty.

This process in Communist totalitarian systems has been specifically linked with the rapid development of an industrial economic order. Communist dictatorships have made industrialization and (to a lesser degree) collectivization the central theme of their internal revolution, partially to prove ex post facto the correctness of Marxist assumptions, partially because, in a technological age, industry is the backbone of national power, and especially because they seized power in backward areas where industrial development had been seriously retarded but had become the focal point of aspirations. Industrialization, imposed politically and without regard to cost, not only necessitates great sacrifices from the people, but also involves the application of tremendous coercive force on those who, because of tradition, self-interest, or apathy, resist it. In that sense, Soviet terror in the 1930's was functionally rational, although its aberrations and excesses were frequently irrational. Some theorists have tended, however, to overemphasize the latter aspects. The oppression and terror of the Soviet system was significantly linked with this ruthless attempt, at all costs, to destroy the existing way of life. It involved the commitment of all the energies of the regime to push the program and mobilize the entire population to carry it through.

The first repercussions of this program were therefore in the direction of accentuating the totalitarian character of the system. As industrialization and collectivization through coercion grew in scope, an increasing number of people were affected. Traditional allegiances and alliances were shattered, and those suspected of opposing the Party program were arrested, deported, or shot. Terror and fear grew rapidly. Not even the Party was immune, and countless members were purged for alleged inefficiency, often translated into accusations of sabotage and wrecking.[4] The first consequences of industrialization, to repeat, were thus to maximize existing fear, arbitrariness, caprice, and terror—in other words, to stress the irrational elements. At the same time, a tremendous social upheaval was created, and literally millions of people were torn from their traditional occupations or surroundings. While this meant misery or death for many, it also opened up unprecedented opportunities for rapid advancement. The totalitarian revolution, therefore, not only stimulated negative reactions; it appealed to the imaginations and self-interest of many others. The presence in this upheaval of a disciplined, and the only organized, body, the Communist Party, gave its leaders almost unlimited power to channel the revolution, to direct it, to head it. A society in this stage of destruction and construction could not produce any restraints on the totalitarian leadership. A society subjected to so total a revolution, socially and economically, offers only two political alternatives: anarchy or totalitarian control. The disciplined and militant totalitarian movement ensured the latter alternative.

We do not know what forms the totalitarian revolution, unhindered externally, would have taken in the more advanced societies where totalitarian movements came to power before World War II. Those, like Poland and Czechoslovakia, that have come under Communist dictatorships since the war have in a broad sense been subjected to the same pattern, although with significant variations pointing in the direction of greater gradualism. Nonetheless, collectivization, nationalization of trade, and expansion of heavy industry all have tended to reproduce this total social impact that dissolves the traditional society. Very specific circumstantial factors prevented the Fascist and Nazi regimes from launching similar large-scale schemes of social reconstruction. Nonetheless, it is sufficient to read Starace's plans to change the Italian national character or Mussolini's remarks on the need to eradicate the Italian "softness," as well as some of the Party regulations on daily behavior of the citizen issued in 1938, to realize that such a revolution was being seriously contemplated in Italy. In the case of the Nazis, there is even more ample evidence that the New Order in Europe would have resulted in revolutionary changes in Germany proper, changes highly inimical to the established order. Hitler's wartime conversations and Himmler's plans for the SS are full of projects that would have involved radical changes in German society and economy.

The question arises, however, as to what happens when the initial impetus of purposefully induced change has spent itself. What happens when the initial economic drive is more or less achieved, and further efforts are merely the accentuation of something already existing?

A RATIONALIST TOTALITARIANISM?

It could be argued, and some have, that Soviet totalitarianism, the most advanced totalitarian society of our age, is now entering upon a new stage of development, the character of which will be determined by the industrialized nature of the Soviet economy. This analysis, partaking somewhat of a material determinism, stresses the incompatibilities between totalitarianism and the requirements of a modern, industrial, and hence also bureaucratic order. Noting that totalitarianism in the past has seemed largely irrational, it argues that the rationalistic routines of the indispensable managers of the industrial society will necessarily transmit themselves to the totalitarian leadership and gradually effect a fundamental transformation of the system itself. This transmission will be aided by the fact that the totalitarian movement has become highly bureaucratized and therefore shares in many of the operational patterns associated with running the industrial machine. Furthermore, it is argued, the totalitarian movement itself has increasingly become staffed by the managerial-bureaucratic elements to whom Party membership means no more than an important club association necessary to satisfy career ambitions. The revolutionary torch and the unending quest are accordingly displaced by the swivel chair and the time clock.

Totalitarianism, in the extreme form of this argument, is thus to disappear imperceptibly and unintentionally. As stability, predictability, and over-all rationality set in, fear, terror, and arbitrariness will fade. Mass enthusiasm and passionate unanimity will give way to disagreements on matters of expertise, and hence also on policy. Policy discussion will then become genuine arguments on alternate courses of action; selection will be made on the basis of rational (technical, objective assessments of the implications of perceived reality) considerations without violent (hence arbitrary and fear-inspiring) consequences for those whose arguments did not prevail. This, together with the growing stability of various privilege groups, will in turn lead to a form of pluralism, suggestive of the existing democratic systems. Democracy, even though likely a curtailed one, will enter by the back door.

One example of this type of reasoning is the argument advanced by Deutscher. He stresses the point that "the economic progress made during the Stalin era has at last brought within the reach of the people a measure of well-being which should make possible an orderly winding up of Stalinism and a gradual democratic evolution." [5] This argument leaves considerable room for dissent. Democracy involves more than what Deutscher suggests. It requires, in the view of some, a certain philosophical tradition, a basic recognition of some sort of higher law, a fundamental attitude of toleration, an absence of doctrinal fanaticism—all of which are, at most, only indirectly linked to a state of "well-being," and none of which seem to be even remotely present in the existing Soviet scene. One may also wonder what is actually meant by "a measure of well-being," especially since wants are relative. Furthermore, there is little of substance in what is known today of totalitarian institutions to indicate the likelihood of such a democratic development. It is difficult to assume that the Party, having such a vested interest, will be willing to resign its absolute control of the instruments of power. The argument also assumes a short-range quality to the goals of the Party, and it ignores the impact of international developments on domestic policies. Deutscher's analysis thus falls down on two counts: Its highly monistic interpretation of democracy fails to see democratic development in its complex and pluralistic perspective, the economic aspects of which are merely one component part of a diversified whole; and its interpretation of Soviet totalitarianism fails to perceive the self-generating power of the system of controls and the resulting vested interests in the maintenance of these controls.

The question remains, however, whether in the long run totalitarianism is compatible with a rationalistic orientation prevailing in its extensive bureaucracy and in the managerial classes of its industrial order. To some extent, this issue, like the one discussed above, is made more complex by the general problem of the range of predictability in political science. It is doubtful that any "scientific" prediction can be made in matters not clearly connected with institutional, legal, stable processes—such as, for instance, one that Presidential elections will occur in the United States in 1964 and 1968, and that, barring some drastic denouement, the contenders will be the Democratic and Republican parties. Predictability becomes more difficult, and its range much shorter, in matters involving general problems of political-social development in a system where little is known of the

28

processes of decision-making at the top, of the motivations and considerations involved, of the nature of the various power alignments, and, last but not least, of the morale of the leaders. There are also few biographical data, beyond the barest essentials, about most of the leaders. In such cases, one must rely to a considerable degree on the projection of past experience, and estimate the future implications of current commitments of the system.

The experience of Germany with Nazi totalitarianism, albeit brief, may therefore not be irrelevant. The Nazi system was imposed with all the earmarks of revolutionary totalitarianism on a society with a highly developed industrial order, with an established and conservative managerial class, with the most efficient and routinized bureaucracy in all Europe. Yet there is no indication in all the available evidence that the fanatical, often irrational, and usually brutal Nazi leadership was in any way deterred from its purposes by the influence or orientations of the German technocrats and bureaucrats. With few exceptions, the bureaucrats and technocrats adjusted meekly to the requirements of the totalitarian movement and were happy to reap any material benefits that Nazi successes produced. It was not until the Nazi regime began to crumble that the bureaucratic and technocratic elements (e.g., Speer) showed any initiative or purposeful action of their own. Until then, it was more a matter of the bureaucrats absorbing Nazi values (e.g., in the treatment of slave laborers) than of the Nazis absorbing a bureaucratic orientation. It seems, therefore, that a violent, arbitrary totalitarianism can, at least, arise and maintain itself in an industrially advanced area without loss of its revolutionary zeal and fanatic brutality. It did so in Germany, Italy, and Czechoslovakia.* The crucial factor throughout was the presence of a movement with a revolutionary morale able to wield effectively the instruments of power.

A rebuttal might point, however, to the facts that both the German and Italian systems were of brief duration and that the experience of Czechoslovakia is too recent for confident evaluation. Furthermore, the emergence of a new and imposing industrial and bureaucratic order under the totalitarian regime itself in the U.S.S.R. is obviously of the greatest importance for the domestic political development of the Soviet society. It is a development not paralleled in any of the other countries mentioned, where the totalitarian movements were superimposed on already existing industrial systems.

One must acknowledge, therefore, that conceivably totalitarianism may become, because of the factors suggested and in spite of the Nazi experience, rationalistic and hence less unpredictable, arbitrary and openly terroristic. But there is no evidence to suggest that this in itself is incompatible with totalitarianism, which need not be interpreted in terms of irrational terror almost for the sake of terror. Such a rationalist system, arising in the context of one-party domination (not to mention international pressures), could be nothing less than a rationalist

---

* There is also the case of Japan, where industrialization advanced rapidly under a form of government increasingly marked by totalitarian tendencies. All indications prior to 1945 suggested that a "democratic evolution" was not to be expected.

dictatorship, just as total in control as its less predictable and more violent antecedent of the 1930's. The institutionalized revolution that still characterizes the existing totalitarianisms will inevitably slow down in the future, but by then it will be involved in an economic commitment that also has its own political logic. The totalitarian economy, as many have observed, has been developed in the U.S.S.R. over the last thirty-five years in keeping with plans oriented to a final (if not yet precisely defined) goal. It is thus a goal-oriented economy, the goal being Communism. That this goal needs more definite formulation is, for our purposes, irrelevant. The important thing is that those in charge of the Soviet society have assumed that economic and social development in all its aspects can be purposefully steered by man in the direction of an ideal solution. This produces consequences that are not only economic but also political, quite different from those induced by other equally technologically advanced economic systems where, to a large extent, economic life is self-directive and ultimate goals, such as plenty and progress, are purposely vague. These goals have less bearing on current decisions than such factors as past experience, demand, prices, competition, and opportunity. In the latter case, a measure of freedom of interplay is inherent. In the former, all decisions and plans are made, or are rationalized, in terms of the ultimate goal.

Consequently, it makes little *political* difference whether the range of man's alternatives is limited by uneducated revolutionaries or by scientific Ph.D.'s, once the entire economy is subjected to a process of human engineering oriented on a goal that cannot be questioned. Admittedly, operations conducted by trained bureaucrats and techno-crats may be more rational and less directly oppressive (insofar as extreme oppression may be uneconomical, which is not entirely certain). But to be less totalitarian, such operations would have to involve some degree of withdrawal on the part of those in charge from their com-mitment to total social and economic engineering, thus granting to those living under the system the opportunity to make important choices *not* in keeping with the goal. But such a politically meaningful development would, in turn, involve a further condition, which at present ap-pears highly unlikely—namely, the decline of ideology and a basic reconsideration of the firmly instituted schemes of economic development. Barring that, the totalitarian economic system would continue to exert pressures for the maintenance of a dictatorship capable of enforcing the kind of discipline that such total plans demand. It is doubtful that, as long as the Party remains in power, the tendency of the regime to stress unattainable goals will vanish. Indeed, it is these goals, inherent in the current ideology, that justify to the population the sacrifices the Party's domination involves. Thus, as long as the Party continues to hold its successful grip on the instruments of power, we can expect it to continue stressing, first, the long-range goals of an ultimate utopia, and then the con-sequent sacrifices to achieve them, even though possibly at a diminishing rate of effort.*

The rationalist tomorrow, if it ever comes, will there-fore not be an introduction to a democratic form of

---

* The most recent illustration of this is the extensive program adopted by the Twenty-second CPSU Congress in 1961.

government, but rather a stage in further totalitarian evolution, accentuating rationalist features present from the start and minimizing some of the irrational outbursts already noted. The prototypes of such a rationalist totalitarianism need not be sought only in Orwell's *1984*. They exist, in an embryonic stage, in our own industrial organizations and bureaucracies. If one could imagine the entire United States run like some executive department, with its myriad of minute, and often incomprehensible, regulations, routinized procedures, even sometimes arbitrariness of officials, one would be all the more inclined to be thankful that the rule of law (rooted in a traditional regard for the individual) and legislative fears of administrative expansion (a democratic "irrationalist" feature) act as a check.[6]

Totalitarianism and rationality, therefore, when viewed in a developmental perspective and not merely from a standpoint of a static definition pinpointing certain characteristics of a given epoch, are not necessarily incompatible. Rationality alone is hardly a sufficient condition for the inevitable growth of a democratic order. At different stages, totalitarianism can be characterized by a minimization of rationalist considerations (as in the 1930's in the U.S.S.R. and in China more recently) or by an increased emphasis on them. But it is as unlikely that totalitarianism can become fully rational as it is incorrect to claim that it has been essentially irrational in the past. Today, for instance, in the U.S.S.R. the totalitarian system is operating in an environment where the need (as seen by the leadership) for unbridled violence, terror in its most open form, and unpredictability based on dictatorial whims seems no longer to be present or desirable. The population appears to be relatively pliant, the younger generation has absorbed a great deal of the indoctrination, and resistance of an active kind is almost entirely absent. The domination of the Party in the country, and of the leadership in the Party, appears to be firmly established. If only the Party could be satisfied with the status quo, a rationalist totalitarianism could possibly become reality.

But even then the problem of power would not disappear. Governmental rationality cannot go far beyond the realm of function and account for all human action. Basic drives for power are not likely to wane. And given the nature of the system, even if the Party declines and is supplanted ultimately by the bureaucracy (or merges with it), the total control of the system over those under it will not disappear even though its exercise will become more functionally rational. In such a system, it is likely that the institutional controls will be utilized to maintain the existing interests of the ruling class, and social stratification will become even more marked as position, education, and even wealth become inheritable. The abyss between those wielding power and the masses will create a real ruling caste, which itself will be highly stratified in terms of the proximity of its members to the center of power. It will create, too, an entire nonpolitical stratum of those who will be given a vested interest in the status quo by virtue of their utility to the system, such as the specialists, artists, military scientists, etc. In many respects, such a system will more nearly resemble the Nazi-Fascist dictatorship than the earlier Stalinist model. This curiously dialectical consequence might deprive Soviet totalitarianism of its revolutionary essence while maintaining its institutional forms. The lesson of history, however, is that this does not necessarily spell the end of the system.

But at best, that appears to be only a distant prospect. The tasks that face the totalitarians today in the captive nations in Europe, among the long dormant masses of China, in the rice paddies of North Vietnam, or in the Malayan jungles—not to speak of the virgin lands, overgrown urban centers, and ever-struggling collective farms in the U.S.S.R.—are very difficult and likely to command all their energies for many years to come. Indeed, the commitments currently made by the present Soviet leaders indicate that the Party is not satisfied with the status quo; hence the abandonment of large-scale drives, which involve in turn the maintenance of discipline, does not seem imminent even in the U.S.S.R., the most developed totalitarian system. These commitments are both domestic and international. Domestically, they suggest a three-pronged attack on the following goals: an increased emphasis on Party zeal, especially in terms of a reassertion of Leninism as defined by the present leadership; continued expansion of industry with major goals set for 1970; further drives in the agricultural sector, including both reclamation projects and the diminution of private plots. On the international plane, briefly, the commitments made to China and the satellites, coupled with those now being made to the underdeveloped countries, will continue to be felt on the domestic scene through scarcities and insistence on maximum effort. At the same time, with Stalin dead and Stalinism impracticable without him, the new leadership is searching for a new basis for power in the realm of both ideological justification and practical measures. This already has meant the rejection of some of the vicious attributes of Stalinism as well as an attack on Stalin himself. It involved in turn some unsettling consequences, as an accepted frame of reference was destroyed and old slogans and operational procedures fell by the wayside. Finally, the problem of succession, given the ages of the present leaders, cannot be dismissed as having been resolved entirely. From all this, it might appear therefore that both internally and externally the likelihood of a status quo situation in the foreseeable future is doubtful. If so, the era of revolutionary totalitarianism may not yet be over.

2. Patterns of Autocracy

Executive power combines policy-making with the direction of policy execution. It is this combination that endows the executive organ in the governmental structure with its crucial functional importance and vests it, or rather the persons who symbolize or control it, with the mystique normally surrounding a head of state or a monarch. In the minds of most people, a president, a king, or even a premier—and today, in one third of the globe, a First Secretary of the Party—plays the role of leader, much in the tradition of the family head, the village elder, or the tribal chief.

Through the ages, society has depended on the chief executives for a sense of direction, and they have stood at the apex of the social and political hierarchy whenever necessity has forced men to band together. Executive power may, in fact, be the oldest and the most necessary social institution in the world. It has taken many forms, has been established through diverse channels ranging from birth to purposely perpetrated death, and has been invested with different ranges of authority at various places and times and in response to varying requirements. Nonetheless, for our purposes it might be useful to distinguish in broad terms between the two types of executive power usually found since the rise of the modern state: the constitutional and the autocratic.

Constitutional executive power, of somewhat more recent vintage and normally a product of a more sophisticated stage of social, cultural, and political development, generally involves an executive organ operating within confines delimited by an institutional structure in which the executive power is both shared with other governmental organs and restricted, even within its own sphere, by a series of formal and informal restraints. The most classical sharing of power is, of course, that involving its division into the executive, legislative, and judicial branches, each relatively free from the domination of the other. There are legal restraints on the arbitrary exercise of power, as well as those inherent in the pluralistic character of modern society which produce their own shifting patterns of social alliances, pressure groups, and veto groups. In such a context, the executive power, while not deprived of its functional significance, is prevented from becoming the dominant and relatively unrestrained source of political leadership.

The autocratic executive, by way of contrast, is relatively unhindered in the exercise of its power and does not share it with other organs, such as the judiciary or the legislature, since they are either absent or subordinate to the executive. Formal restraints, such as legal injunctions, also are either absent or circumvented, while informal restraints—for example, those involving the church as a major institution—are somewhat more elastic in the assertion of their claims against the executive. In brief, the autocratic executive is the central, dominant, and leading governmental organ.

It should further be noted that the autocratic form of executive power is in many ways the older and more basic of the two types. The much more complex constitutional form has arisen only under certain favorable conditions of social stability and economic well-being, and under the guidance of an enlightened elite. Such conditions have not been as frequent as might be desired. A mere glance at the political history of mankind reveals that most people have lived under some sort of autocratic (that is to say, nonresponsible and nonrepresentative) form of government.

The above observation is pertinent to the problem of continuity and discontinuity in the Russian executive in the years since 1861. Throughout the century (with one brief interlude, measured not in years but in mere months), the Russian executive has been an essentially autocratic one.* As we shall see, however, within this dominant autocratic pattern, varying degrees of intensity and directions of change have been discernible.

AUTOCRATIC TRADITION

The autocratic character of the Russian executive during most of the last century, with the consequently important element of continuity, can be brought out in sharper

* More will be said later about the implications and nature of the Duma period just prior to World War I. It is not possible, in this brief space, to present both a detailed institutional account of the roles played by the Czarist and Soviet executives and a meaningful analysis of their continuities and discontinuities. I will concentrate on the latter and merely point to certain relevant institutional aspects.

focus if we attempt to examine more closely some of the salient features of the Czarist and Soviet executives to see how they show a definite perpetuation in autocratic pattern. What have been some of the important political characteristics of the Russian executive during this period?

To a political observer, the concentration of power in the executive organ to the detriment of the judicial or legislative bodies might well be the crucial criterion. The supreme authority of the Russian emperor as the autocrat was acknowledged by basic law and cemented by tradition. This supreme power was exercised on the emperor's behalf and at his will by ministers selected, appointed, and dismissed by him. These ministers were sometimes headed by an informal chairman of the ministerial council who, at least nominally, was the emperor's closest adviser.

However, unlike Western practice, it was always the emperor, and not the chairman (a post not regularized until the twentieth century), who personally selected and nominated the members of the ministerial committee. Thus, even the element of indirect restraint on the emperor—inherent in the cabinet system, in which the ministers developed a measure of institutional authority of their own—was absent in this case. As a result, cabinet ministers did not feel compelled to coordinate their operations with the chairman of their council, and they rarely met in a body. The normal practice was for the emperor to closet himself with especially trusted ministers and to decide in this small group what the policy on an issue ought to be.

In the case of the more important policy posts, such as foreign affairs or defense, the ministers dealt directly with the emperor, even as late as the twentieth century, when the practice of appointing a premier became institutionalized.* Count Kokovtsov, Premier under Nicholas II, recalled with a touch of bitterness how the Minister of Internal Affairs neglected to keep him abreast of developments and how the Minister of War obtained funds for the ministry without even consulting with the Prime Minister.[1] Of course, a particularly strong-willed chairman such as Stolypin could resist these tendencies. However, it was not the general pattern. As a result of this poor bureaucratic coordination at the top governmental levels, matters of high policy involving the executive power were resolved through the direct intervention of the emperor, to whom the central governmental organs— the Ministerial Committee, the Council of the Empire,

---

* In the late nineteenth century, the Committee of Ministers was composed of the following: War and Navy, Finance, Interior, Communications, State Domains, Education, Justice, Foreign Affairs, and Control. The Ministry of the Interior was probably the most important ministry for domestic matters, not only directing the state bureaucracy but, in a sense, setting the broad patterns of domestic policy. It frequently competed for power and prestige with the Finance Ministry, which shaped fiscal policy. Budgetary provisions for the respective ministries suggest their relative weights (except for the Foreign Ministry, the importance of which was less dependent on the vastness of its bureaucratic apparatus). Thus, for instance, in 1887, the expenditures of the Ministry of War and Navy were 251 million rubles; Finance, 109 million; Interior, 73 million; Communications, 26 million; State Domains, 23 million; Education, 21 million; Justice, 20 million; Foreign Affairs, 5 million; Control, 3 million. (See C. Skalkovsky, *Les Ministres des Finances de la Russie* [Paris, 1891], p. 292.) In the case of the War Ministry, many of the expenditures were for the construction of strategically important railroads that were otherwise nonprofitable.

the Senate, and the Holy Synod*—were directly subordinate.

The personal power of the emperor also was enhanced by the monarch's practice of relying on a coterie of personal favorites who often were appointed to fill chief governmental posts. These appointments did not neces-sarily involve men distinguished by a specialized knowl-edge of a particular aspect of government, but instead went to persons considered as personally loyal to the emperor and to the general orientation he held at the time, whether liberal or conservative. As a result, the emperor became the focal point for competing groups: Those in favor of reforms and those against change felt that their objectives could be achieved only if the emperor could be induced to make his appointments accordingly. Growing political conflict thus advanced the political influence of the emperor, since reform, of whatever kind, could be achieved only with him and through him.

An additional factor in the autocratic pattern was the device of parallel informal and formal channels of execu-tive power. Apart from his chosen ministers—whom the emperor would begin to suspect after a while of harbor-ing views alien to him (views that, in fact, the ministers

* The Council of the Empire, which in the mid-1880's had sixty-four members, was a consultative body for legislative matters. Its members, appointed by the Czar, were usually members of the Imperial family, former and present ministers, and distinguished servants of the Czar. The Senate, likewise composed of appointed dignitaries, was to be the highest judicial body, a court of cassation, and the supreme body for adjudicating administrative conflicts. One of its seven departments also handled governmental auditing. The Holy Synod, headed by a lay procurator general and composed of the metropolitans and bishops, dealt with religious matters as well as general problems of state morality.

frequently acquired by being brought into contact with the realities of Russia once they were appointed to cope with them)—the emperor would consult special advisers not burdened with executive posts. These would most frequently be drawn from among his personal courtiers, many of whom held high military ranks and were his devoted and disciplined servants, jealously protecting his power but often suffering from a lack of native intelligence.[2]

The most notable exceptions in this period to the pattern of courtier-advisers were Pobedonostsev and Rasputin, though the latter was influential through the empress.[3] Pobedonostsev's relationship with Alexander III is particularly illustrative of the role played by *éminences grises* in autocratic regimes. His influence had a far wider range than was justified by his post of Procurator General of the Holy Synod. He was Alexander's adviser on important matters of policy and a vigorous defender of the Czar's power against real and imagined encroachments on the part of those allegedly favoring constitutionalism. He effectively torpedoed Loris-Melikov's cautious reforms and successfully urged the Czar to replace Loris-Melikov with a more rigid minister. Pobedonostsev's correspondence with the emperor, in which he skillfully exploited the prejudices of this intellectually limited monarch— who was fearful of further reforms and mindful of the assassination of his father—and his personal intrigues, his little coups, his distrust of intellectuals, and his general philosophical position [4] immediately bring to mind an analogy with Stalin. Pobedonostsev combined in one person Stalin's Poskrebyshev (whom Khrushchev sarcastically dubbed Stalin's "loyal shield-bearer" in his 1956 "secret speech") and Zhdanov, but without the latter's political role and position as erstwhile heir-apparent. He provided the monarch with informal sources of information and served as his ideologue, his chief defender and rationalizer of the status quo.*

Soviet political practices have not, on the whole, deviated significantly from the pattern sketched above. Throughout most of the political history of the Soviet Union, one-man rule has been the norm, and recent events do not augur an imminent departure from long-established practice. Indeed, it has been argued cogently that a system such as the Soviet one cannot operate without producing overwhelming internal pressures toward the elevation of some individual to the top of the political structure. Furthermore, Soviet political leaders have come not from the ranks of the administrators but from the Party, which endows them with a certain aura of "scientific" insight into history, analogous to the personal charisma of the anointed emperor.

---

* It is interesting to reflect that Pobedonostsev's insistence on a rigid system based on law strongly suggests that his ideal would have been the Platonic society, with its reliance on state religion, family training, indoctrination of the intellectual—all within a firm legal framework. These were precisely the things that Pobedonostsev was advocating and, in some measure, implementing. However, judging by his criticisms of the idea of a search for truth, one might speculate that the *Laws*, rather than the *Republic*, would have been more to his liking. For some discussions of his views, see A. A. Kornilov, *Kurs istorii Rossii XIX veka* (Moscow, 1918), III, 269; and R. F. Byrnes, "Pobedonostsev on the Instruments of Russian Government," in Ernest J. Simmons (ed.), *Continuity and Change in Russian and Soviet Thought* (Cambridge, Mass.: Harvard University Press, 1955).

The Party secretaries, while not ignoring the significant role played by the bureaucrats, have maintained the tradition of keeping the administrators tied to administrative procedures and have retained policy-making as their own domain, to be shared with those of their own choosing. It was only following Stalin's assumption of the Premiership that the Party and the administration came to be closely linked at the top. But even throughout the Stalinist period, which was marked by a growing ascendancy of the administrative structure, little doubt remained as to which post was politically the more important. Khrushchev's career is mute testimony to this point.

While coordination of decision-making has probably improved since the Czarist days, there is no doubt that problems of policy are still resolved by informal cabals of "politicians" and not by administrators: Stalin with Poskrebyshev and Malenkov for administrative-personnel matters, Zhdanov for ideological issues, and his more trusted Politburo members (depending on the dictator's whims) for broader consultation; and Khrushchev with his reliable *apparatchiki* as the source of necessary support and counsel and sometimes as the manpower for important administrative appointments. Given the voluminous literature on Soviet politics, these brief observations may suffice to suggest some strong parallels with the previously outlined pattern of Czarist executive power.

Another important area of political relationships pertinent to this investigation involves the related questions of political centralization and political coercion. While the latter does not necessarily follow from the former (as with France), there is a strong tendency in regimes that are not constitutionally based for the two to merge. This was the case under the Czars, and it is the case today in Soviet Russia.

In Czarist Russia, centralization and coercion took the form of strict subordination of local authority (such as the *Gubernator,* the *Gradonachal'nik,* or, since 1889, the *Zemskii nachal'nik,* as well as the *Stanovoi,* the *Ispravnik,* and the *Uriadnik*) to the Minister of the Interior,[5] and the employment of centrally controlled police power for political ends. Of course, a particularly dynamic governor could achieve a certain amount of autonomy, especially in an outlying region, but usually by virtue of his ability to anticipate the desiderata of St. Petersburg and to execute them even more efficiently than anticipated.* In this sense, there is a strong resemblance to the able and energetic Stalinist satraps in the republics—people like Bagirov, for instance, who held his post for some fifteen years without interruption. However, centralization normally breeds overbureaucratization, and the Russian local officials were frequently swamped with dreary paperwork and red tape —again much like their Soviet counterparts.[6] A measure of internal decay is a corollary of autocratic bureaucracies.

Political coercion was also a major preoccupation of the

* The check, supposedly provided by the local procurator, subordinated to the Ministry of Justice, unfortunately often proved illusory since the governor normally wielded more influence back in St. Petersburg. Cf. N. Flerovsky, *Tri politicheskiia sistemy* (1897), pp. 54–55. Another check involved the periodic inspections by delegated senators. In a sense, they performed the functions of control somewhat like the Party control commissions or RKI. But again, personal factors were of critical importance.

Russian executive organ, a preoccupation lasting to this day. The police were under the administrative supervision of the Ministry of the Interior, and the chief of police was appointed by the minister, was personally responsible to him, and retired whenever the minister retired. Following the reorganizations of 1880 and 1882, the Assistant Minister of the Interior became the commander of the Special Gendarme Corps, a security formation. The Okhrana, part of the police department of the Ministry of the Interior, provided the intelligence and counter-revolutionary operations. This was the political branch.[7] With the increasing ferment, there was a growing tendency to exempt political cases from judicial "interference" by placing them under the jurisdiction of military courts. Between 1891 and 1901, all political cases were handled by military tribunals, and the extraordinary procedures provided in the decree of August 14, 1881, "Measures for the Preservation of State Order and Tranquillity," were renewed every three years until the fall of Czardom.[8] Death sentences, which (as in Soviet Russia until very recently) were applied only in political cases, for acts undermining the executive power, were imposed with sufficient frequency to underscore the autocratic character of the regime.[9]

A common characteristic of autocratic regimes is the effort on the part of the executive branch to subvert judicial independence for the sake of political ends. In Czarist Russia, this took the form of direct and indirect pressure on judges trying political cases, removal of such cases from the jurisdiction of established tribunals (as indicated above), promulgation of emergency punitive measures (as in 1905), and administrative dispensation of justice.[10]

In the words of the last chief of the Okhrana: "There was only one form of extra-judicial punishment, and that was administrative banishment; sentences of up to five years could be pronounced." He adds that this was "frequently but leniently applied."[11] The absence of a strong legal tradition in Russia facilitated these deviations from the rule of law, which, when firmly rooted, inherently serves as a check on executive power.[12]

The Soviet parallels are self-evident. Political centralization in the U.S.S.R. is achieved, despite constitutional provisions, by the subordination of republican (and lower) organs to the central political administration in Moscow. Beyond that, the Party acts as the chief coordinating instrument and has lately acquired an even more important coordinating capacity as a result of the economic reorganization. Soviet archives, such as the Smolensk *Obkom* and *Oblispolkom*,[13] leave little doubt that, underneath fictitious lip service to federalism and the importance of local initiative, central executive control is indisputable and has been so during the entire Soviet period, despite some modest efforts during the NEP to give meaning to republican autonomy. Organized violence, to protect the Soviet form of government and hence to destroy all real and potential opponents, has been associated from the very beginning with central executive power and has not been impeded by excessive judicial sensitivity on the part of the Soviet leaders. Vishinsky's

48

statement that "the contents and form of judicial activities cannot avoid being subordinated to political class aims and strivings"[14] still holds today, even though its author may have been at least partially repudiated. Death penalties for political crimes have been applied more generously than under the Czars, and administrative organs have freely imposed severe penalties on those accused of political offenses. Centralization and coercion continue to be important attributes of the executive in Russia.

One final similarity between the executive organs of Russia before and after the 1917 Revolution lies in an area that is not necessarily characteristic of autocratic regimes, but has been important to the maintenance in power of the Russian regimes. This is the relation of the executive to the military. In many autocratic regimes, political power becomes so dependent on the military establishment that power ultimately passes to the military, or the military, as a group, are continually involved in attempts to "salvage" the national interest. This was not so in Czarist Russia (except for the short and untypical period after 1916) or in Soviet Russia. Apparently, the Russian military leadership—somewhat like the Russian Orthodox Church leaders—has developed a sense of political noninvolvement that makes it difficult for any would-be Bonapartist leader to use the army as a cohesive unit for political purposes. In the case of the Czar, there were the elements of personal loyalty and wise personnel policy: For instance, many high officers occupied influential and lucrative administrative posts. In the U.S.S.R., there may be ideological loyalty, and there is certainly a

49

complex network of police and Party controls and purges. Whatever the technique or causes, the political effect is similar.*

Russian history indicates that a crucial element of continuity in the Russian executive since 1861 has been the almost uninterrupted maintenance of an autocratic pattern of executive power, with the resultant minimization of restraints on the arbitrary exercise of that power. In this sense, the Soviet Union merely follows a trail blazed by centuries of earlier Russian political tradition. But this establishes only the broad outlines of continuity and hardly exhausts our problem. Are historical parallels enough to posit historical continuity?

Totalitarian Innovation

Within the framework of an essentially autocratic pattern, there are significant differences between the Czarist and Soviet executives, both in degree and kind, which demand investigation and theoretical evaluation.

As noted in Chapter 1 (pp. 16–18), there are three broad types of restraints on political power: the direct, the indirect, and the natural. Of these three, the Czarist executive, in the final analysis, effectively subverted only the first,

---

* Of course, there have been plots among younger officers, impatient with the Czarist policy of status quo, such as the Voennaia Organizatsiia Partii Narodnoi Volii. The officers, however, were all of junior rank, and this made it quite impossible to use the Army as a unit for political purposes. These traditional considerations, apart from the more immediately significant factor of highly institutionalized controls and intense indoctrination, might also have been taken into account by those who for the last few years have made a profession out of predicting an imminent takeover of political power in the U.S.S.R. by the military.

sometimes came into conflict with the second, and never challenged the third. Its relationship with the church or the *zemstvos* was one of control, especially in the case of the former; with the growing industrial and middle class, it was, broadly speaking, one of adjustment. As far as the family is concerned, it never went beyond the point reached by most modern states—insistence on education and a degree of patriotic conformity. The Soviets have continued this subversion of the direct restraints, but have gone beyond that in destroying the second kind and effectively challenging, if not entirely overcoming, the third. Thus, we have a broad area in which important differences appear in sharp focus and demand closer scrutiny.

The following question arises: If both executives can be considered autocratic, why is there such variation in the relation between political power and political restraint? The answer is to be found in the nature of the basic attitude of these executives toward the existing society. A traditional regime, with its paternalistic sense of authority, recognizes a transcendent system of values that inherently limits its otherwise institutionally wide scope of action. The Czarist executive was motivated by just such a curious mixture of autocratic paternalism and a strong belief in the immaturity of the people. This frequently made it resort to violence, but never allowed it to seek the logical conclusion of that violence—the complete extermination of its enemies—because of the conscious and unconscious assumptions inherent in the paternalistic attitude. Conflicts that did arise, such as the challenge to the economic interests of the gentry by state-encouraged industrialization or, subsequently, by the

Stolypin reform, were still the result of an attempted response to changes in society and not a matter of preconceived policy of subordinating or destroying rural interest groups for the sake of eliminating restraints on the power of the regime. The powers-to-be in the Czarist executive, ranging from Pobedonostsev or Rasputin to Loris-Melikov or Stolypin, and including the Czars, all shared in the desire to defend the broad outlines of the status quo, although obviously differing on such specific measures as the need for reform or the desirability of reaction. But commitment to the status quo involves a limitation of power by that status quo and a measure of acceptance of its inherent values. If one takes society and the political system as they are, then one's power is fitted into the existing framework of that society, even if such things as law and constitution (direct restraints) are not too vital. The other types of restraints compensate somewhat for this absence of the direct restraints.

The Soviet attitude, motivated by an ideology that puts a premium on *conscious* political action based on a relatively defined and dogmatic action program (qualities lacking in the more general and traditional viewpoints of the Czarist reforms), aims at the transformation of existing society, which it initially rejects. This act of rejection liberates the Soviet leadership from the limitations of the status quo, and the conviction of the Soviet leaders that they possess an insight into the inevitabilities of history justifies all their acts. The reliance on a revolutionary movement, for which there was no parallel in Czarist Russia, gives the Soviet leadership an independent tool for the removal of restraints on its power, even if some bureaucrats (because of their professional interest in a measure of stability) are wary of excessive change. As a result, the power of the executive pervades the entire society, maintaining its grip even as the impetus of the initial blows fades, as the new society begins to take shape and its rulers develop a vested interest in the new status quo. By then, the society has become both molded and penetrated by political organs that parallel the purely administrative structure and give the top executive a significantly greater scope of action. It could even be argued that, at this stage, the distinction that could be made in the case of Czarist Russia between the political system and society becomes meaningless. At the same time, because of the dynamic and ideological quality of the struggle undertaken, the executive is much more conscious of the need to keep its movement vital, especially since the elimination of pluralistic groups tends to give the movement a monopoly of power without the invigorating effect of continuing competition. Purges thus become the inherent device for coping with this situation and maintaining the revolutionary dynamics.

The process of pulverizing society effectively eliminates all political opposition and leads to the mobilization of all social energy for the achievement of the politically defined goals. The result is a far greater pattern of compliance to political power than under the Czarist executive. While many examples could be cited involving such fields as the arts, sciences, or the press (despite censorship, the Czarist press was an example of diversity compared to the Soviet),[15] it may help to review the handling of political cases and the general problem of political opposition to the regime in power. The summary treatment of political opponents by Czarist military tribunals and the relative absence of inhibition with respect to the execution of such opponents has been noted. However, there were also spectacular cases of judicial independence, even in the more violent days of Russian political history. In the trial of Vera Zasulich, the presiding judge, at the risk of prejudicing his future career, effectively resisted political pressure from the executive; the defense made impassioned appeals on behalf of the defendant, and the jury, acting with an overriding sense of justice, acquitted her to the accompaniment of thunderous applause. What a contrast with the behavior of the spectators and the judges in the Hall of Crystals exactly sixty years later! At the nonjury trial of the Czar's assassins (the government had become more cautious), the chief defendant, Zheliabov, unflinchingly defended his position and forcefully demanded that a jury trial be held—behavior not noted in Soviet political cases. Until the collapse of the empire, many defense lawyers courageously and devotedly defended, in many cases successfully, political prisoners accused of subversion or revolutionary activity. Soviet judicial history is not marked by such episodes.

The executive in Russia under the Czars was committed to a defense of a political status quo in which the autocratic power was traditional while the society itself was changing with increasing tempo under the impact of slowly expanding literacy, economic reforms often initiated by the regime itself, growing urban centers, and a spreading consciousness of the need for change. This meant that the regime's security was more and more frequently challenged by revolutionary groups desiring drastic reforms. The executive could not take measures violent enough to uproot and wipe out all opposition without shattering much of the status quo. The absence of technology, while important, was not crucial; certainly, revolutionary regimes in the past (Cromwell or Napoleon) have been able, because of their revolutionary liberation from existing societal limitations, to cope effectively with domestic opposition. As a result, much of the political history of the last few decades of the empire could be written in terms of political plots, conspiracies, assassinations of countless important officials (not to mention the Czar), and intensive revolutionary propaganda.[16] While their political significance should not be exaggerated, they did contribute to the political atmosphere of the time. Pobedonostsev's letter of advice to Alexander III, shortly after Alexander's accession to the throne, catches the atmosphere of internal fear, bred by conspiracy, terror, and ineffectual counterterror:

(1) When you are retiring, Your Majesty, do shut the doors behind you, not only in the bedroom but in all adjoining rooms, the hall included. A trusted person should carefully check the locks and make certain that inside door bars be slid shut. (2) Definitely check every evening before retiring whether bell wires are intact. They can be cut easily. (3) Check every evening underneath the furniture to see whether everything is all right. (4) One of the aides-

de-camp ought to sleep near Your Majesty in the same apartments. (5) Are all persons around Your Majesty trustworthy?[17]

The revolutionaries whom Pobedonostsev feared so—even though they were frequently tracked down, arrested, and executed—combined their revolutionary zeal with a mixture of romanticism and fanaticism that somehow would seem out of place among the current Soviet generation of *tekhnikum* students.[18]

Thus far, the Soviet executive has avoided such a situation by stamping out the opposition while constructing a new society. This revolutionary procedure freed it from traditional limits on power. By the time a new generation grew up, matured, and prepared to take stock (a development delayed by World War II and the Cold War until the mid-1950's), a situation had been created in which opponents of the policies of the present Soviet executive face what might be called "the dilemma of the one alternative." Even if rejecting the system in a personal sense, any critic is forced to admit that by now no meaningful alternatives to it exist. That seems to have been the position of many Soviet students whom I met in the U.S.S.R. in the fall of 1956.

Although a broad pattern of continuity in the autocratic character of the Russian executive is obvious, there is a sharp distinction between the roles played by the Czarist and the Soviet executives. This distinction is inherent in the apparent difference between an autocratic regime based on certain traditional values and generally committed to the status quo, and an autocratic regime revolutionary in its policy and committed ideologically to a radical destruction of the past and long-range programs of utopian reconstruction. Regimes such as the latter have been called totalitarian, and it is this totalitarian development *within* the broad autocratic pattern that reveals a sharp discontinuity in the role and character of the Russian executive since 1861.

CONTINUITY AND CHANGE

A further question now arises. A comparison between the present British Government and that of 1861 would show certain very important differences within the constitutional pattern, leading to the conclusion that a sharp discontinuity is involved. The change from a parliamentary form of government to one that is fundamentally a centralized party form of government might be considered a sharp discontinuity, despite its occurrence within the constitutional pattern. However, continuity and change are in constant interaction, and the present British form of government evolved out of its predecessor. Although the change was gradual, today's government is quite different from what it was in 1861. The question this poses is whether the totalitarian pattern of the present Russian executive was implicit in the gradual changes occurring in the autocratic Czarist executive. If so, then the totalitarian role of the Soviet executive, though different in many respects from the role of the Czarist executive, is nevertheless the natural child of trends implicit in the past.

To examine this position, a review of the confusing

and multidirectional courses pursued by the antecedent regime in Russia might give some indication of a general trend toward patterns of fundamental continuity or proofs of an essential discontinuity. That the record of the Czarist executive was mixed as far as liberalizing and reactionary policies are concerned is clear from a cursory glance at Russian political history. Yet, it also becomes evident that the second half of the nineteenth and the beginning of the twentieth centuries were periods of great changes—changes that might be called spontaneous—in the social and economic life of Russia.

Heavy industry, railroads, and coal and iron complexes were beginning, and the cities reflected the growing opulence and power of a new class of bankers, merchants, and industrialists. These changes, even though they were occurring under the cloak of a political power dusty with antiquated traditions of autocracy, were beginning to make themselves felt. Violent radical conspiracies were their extreme expression. But much more important than these conspiracies was the growing desire of many citizens for reform, for a constitution, for a liberal monarchy.[19] This desire penetrated even the cold walls of the Winter Place, and the emperors gradually found themselves surrounded by whispered, and sometimes loud, warnings that something must be done.

To reform an old autocracy from within is not an easy task. Many vested interests are always against any change other than the natural, imperceptible one. This proved to be so in Russia. Yet, the executive power, which, given the system, was the only effective source of reform, did initiate a number of significant changes. These changes involved not only important areas of the social and economic life of the community, such as the liberation of the peasants or the later Stolypin agricultural reforms, but also political changes that had direct bearing on the power of the executive. The law reform and the organization of jury trial (1864), while still subject to severe limitations in statute and practice,[20] meant that the judicial branch was gradually becoming institutionalized. The law on assemblies, passed in the same year, similarly implied a modest development in the direction of regularized patterns of self-government, albeit on a very limited scale. The press reforms of 1865, the growing vocal activity of the *zemstvos,* and Loris-Melikov's projects were all efforts to bring the autocracy in line with the requirements of the changing society, to bridge the gap between political institutions designed to fight off the Tatar yoke, and to build a society that was now beginning to feel more strongly the impact of growing pains in an age of economic and social revolution.

The dilemma of power in such a context—to liberalize or to contain—meant frequent oscillations and reversals. And yet, even though the executive would shrink back into apparently the only safe refuge of reaction (as in 1882), parts of the society would continue their pressures for change, and the executive would finally respond. But the ambivalence would persist: The Duma period, the desire for a buffer between society and the executive (as explicitly stated by Witte), the electoral reforms would be followed by a relapse, by electoral amendments designed to limit representation by a re-emphasis of Czarist autocracy and by a reassertion of violence, all often welcomed by those who feared change.[21]

Nevertheless, a residue of change would remain and would serve as a springboard for further intensification in the pressures for reform. The development of the prime ministership* and the embryonic growth of a multiparty system were part of institutional changes that even subsequent relapse into reaction could not undo in their entirety. That the change was slow—too slow—seems to have been the final verdict of history, and the regime did not surmount the accumulated pressures when they came to be combined with external blows. However, these considerations still lead one to suggest that the role played by the Soviet executive, given its policies and power, involves a reversal in an admittedly timid and regrettably blurred trend.

In the process of carrying out the Communist revolution, the successor government expanded its powers to a degree unprecedented in modern political history: It reversed the trends toward an independent judiciary, a freer peasantry, and a modest system of political representation based on a pluralistic society. Much of the violence used to build the new Communist society was a product of the need to overcome the inertia that is the usual social response to rapid, purposeful, and ideologically motivated change pushed forward by an organized minority. Much of it was a product of brutal zeal and a lust for power. But one must remember also that the

* The October, 1905, reform formally set up a Council of Ministers, with a prime minister, both modeled on the Western pattern.

terror used by the empire against the revolutionaries in itself contributed to the sharpening of their dogmatic convictions and strengthened their belief in the necessity of violence for the sake of "morally" good ends. This psychological legacy of the empire makes the rulers of the past share responsibility with the rulers of the present for the continued reliance on violence, despite the deep existential and normative differences between the Soviet and Czarist executives.

Recently, there have been some indications that, with a decline in the momentum of internal transformation, voices might be raised inside Russia to dispute the unlimited claim of the executive to rule over the destinies of the Russian people. But the occasional voices of nonconformity are still timid when compared to the literary outcries of the disaffected intellectuals or the heroic declarations of the revolutionary brethren of less than a century ago. The Czarist executive was very gradually, indeed haltingly, moving in the direction of closing the gap between the political regime and society at large by adjusting to the requirements of the society. But it moved too slowly. The Soviet leadership changed society in the image of its own doctrines so that no such gap should exist. The 1957 reforms in the Soviet administrative structure, allegedly granting a greater voice to component federal and economic units, could have been significant in altering the role of the executive and its relation to society. But an element lacking in the empire is now present—the parallel and pervading structure of the Party —and all indications point to the fact that the Party is as powerful as ever. Having surmounted domestic obstacles and being rather optimistic about current world trends, it is not likely to atrophy in the foreseeable future.

Success in itself breeds conservatism and vested interest in the status quo. These, in turn, gradually involve restraints on power, especially as an industrializing society becomes more complex and literate. But neither industrialism nor education is incompatible with totalitarian autocracy. The former breeds pressures for central control and direction; the latter, popular slogans to the contrary, is *divisible* and subject to manipulative controls that stress only those aspects compatible with totalitarian demands and de-emphasize those that are not. Scientific training unaccompanied by the humanities does not inevitably come into conflict with a totalitarian regime that puts a premium on scientific achievement and gives it every opportunity for development. Furthermore, modern scientific education, by being dependent on specialization instead of fostering a true spirit of inquiry, can also be used to promote the acceptance of certain purposes and to instill a peculiar perspective that increases the power of the regime, by making it accepted. A commitment to science or to industrial technology and management, especially if accompanied by a system of high rewards, can be used as effective blinders to social dilemmas and political questions.

Beyond this, given the situation in the U.S.S.R. as well as in the Communist camp in general, a myriad of decisions which are essentially political will have to be made and will require an elite with political skill and a sense of purpose. Since a screening process for promoting such an elite has been developed over the long period dominated by Stalinism, we can expect that for many years to come only dedicated "politicians," or those who successfully pretend that they are, will rise in the hierarchy and ultimately shape decisions. Even if partially due to mere inertia, motivation for such decisions is thus likely to continue stressing common ideologically defined purposes. Considering their revolutionary character and fundamental commitment to struggle, such purposes are bound to cultivate a profound hostility toward even incipient manifestations of social pluralism, without which effective restraints on political power cannot develop.

3. The Nature of the Soviet System

> If the mind is obligated to obey the word of command, it can at any rate feel that it is not free. But if it has been so manipulated beforehand that it obeys without even waiting for the word of command, it loses even the consciousness of enslavement—André Gide.

All modern societies involve mass manipulation, especially since the masses have now become economically and politically important. Whether it is an election or merely a matter of consumption, the crucial factor is the behavior of the activated mass. Motivational research and public-opinion polls are ways of gauging the anticipated reactions of the consumer and the voter. The asymmetry in decision-making between the masses and the businessman or the politician is thus diminished.

But Gide (in the above quotation) had something far more ominous in mind. He was pointing to the possibility of a society's maintaining total political-social conformity, not just with the leadership anticipating the mass reactions, but with the masses, in effect, almost anticipating the desires of the leadership. A self-enforcing unanimity and conformity would be the consequence. But for such a condition to arise, there would have to be some overt, systematized framework of socially instilled values that could guide—almost without command—the behavior of the masses. And if that were to come to pass, perhaps one would be safer not to raise the baffling question of whether such a society were, in fact, free or enslaved. By comparison, Nazi Germany and Soviet Russia of the 1930's and China of today would be examples of admirably simple tyrannies, with the continuous use of force leaving little doubt as to the internal essence of their systems.

ORGANIZATIONAL COMPULSION FOR IDEOLOGY-ACTION

The most prevalent political system has always been some form of authoritarianism, although the scope of arbitrary power has often varied, depending on circumstances, local traditions, the nature of social-political alliances supporting a given regime, and the vitality of institutional and legal customs. Furthermore, with very few exceptions, such regimes have tended to be conservative, usually adopting major reforms only in response to social-economic pressures or political unrest, but rarely actually initiating them. In the event of occasional reform drives, the usual pattern has been one of temporary bursts of initiative, followed by lengthier relapses into conservative passivity.

Regimes of this sort could endure as long as the majority of the population remained politically neutral and passive. A variety of well-known factors undermined this neutrality and passivity. Rapid social-economic changes brought about by the machine age, increased literacy, and the rise of nationalism have contributed to the politicizing of the masses and have made the politics of mass consciousness a feature of our age. Practically all contemporary leaders have to appeal to popular sentiments and organize various forms of mass action in order to wield power effectively.

The extent of the appeal and the manipulation depends on the nature of the objective for which power is wielded and on the susceptibility of the given society to a more or less extensive domination of the masses by an elite. When widespread social disintegration because of war or social-economic crises occurs, the opportunities for the emergence of extremist elites and for the direct domination of the masses are greatest. The weakening (and/or disappearance) of intermediary pluralistic forms of social organization allows for the consolidation of centralized power and for the eventual use of that power to effect large-scale societal reconstruction. To do the latter, both the ruling elite (organized into a revolutionary movement) and the masses must share certain general notions of what was wrong with the past society, as well as an action program for the building of a better one.

The political systems established by such revolutionary movements differ profoundly from old-fashioned dictatorships. Instead of using societal pluralism to manipulate various interests in order to maintain power, these movements take advantage of the occasional weakness of such pluralist groups to seize power and use it first to eliminate all intermediary groups, and then to construct a new society, reflecting the movement's ideology. Such elimination can take place with particular thoroughness and intensity if the given society happens to have lagged behind in the process of modernization. In that case, the construction of a new order can be linked to rapid social-economic and technical development. Today, force and progress make a formidable combination.

Because of the unprecedented total social impact of these regimes, they have been labeled "totalitarian." The word is used to suggest that at some point the scope of arbitrary power and the domination of society by a political elite, especially one that tolerates no barriers between itself and the population, becomes so extensive that differences of degree become differences of kind. Although it is often difficult to define that point with great precision (as is also true in defining "democracies"; for example, is Mexico or France a democracy?), it may be suggested that the totalitarian systems differ in kind from other forms of authoritarian regimes—traditional dictatorships, what has been called the "totalitarian elements in pre-industrial societies,"[1] or the contemporary nationalist single-party regimes—because: (1) their ideology provides a total critique of the antecedent form of societal organization and a prescription for a complete reconstruction of society and man; (2) the absolutist character of their ideology frees the movements of any moral or traditional-legal restraints on their power, and they consider themselves justified in undertaking even the most ruthless steps to consolidate their power and execute their ideology; (3) the combination of these two factors, linked with the urgent belief of the committed members, produces within the movement an *organizational compulsion* for ideologically focused and compatible action (ideology-action) to absorb and/or destroy all social groups that might even constitute passive obstructions to the movement's dynamic need to subordinate society totally to its power. This organizational compulsion absorbs both the leadership and the membership. A good negative example is the difficulty encountered by Lenin in trying to effect a temporary truce between his ruling party and Russian society; the built-in pressure toward action that was felt so acutely within the Soviet Communist Party in the mid-1920's may be seen as a positive example.

The Soviet system has now existed for over forty-four years, and its political history has been closely identified with three major Communist leaders, each symbolizing a distinct but related, stage of development of that system. Broadly speaking, the phase of Leninism after 1917 can be said to have involved primarily the consolidation of the Communist Party's rule over society and the internal transformation of the Party from a revolutionary vanguard into a more disciplined ruling elite. While some small measure of internal diversity remained within the Party, especially at the top, perhaps the most enduring achievement of Leninism was the dogmatization of the Party, which in effect both prepared and caused the next stage, Stalinism.

The Stalinist phase, particularly during the years 1928–41, was the time of what might be called the totalitarian "break-through"—that is, the all-out effort to destroy the basic institutions of the old order and to construct at least the framework for the new. The postwar period, 1945–53, was in some respects a repetition and extension of the preceding period. The process of postwar reconstruction once again meant a conflict with society, destruction of established ways, and an extension of earlier efforts to build "socialism" in agriculture, through industrialization, in the arts and sciences, etc. The political consequence of these efforts, as well as of Stalin's own personality, was a decline in the importance of the Party, the personalization of leadership, the growth of the secret police, and the dominating role of terror as the crucial, most characteristic feature of the system. Indeed, Stalin's totalitarian edifice could be said to have rested on three supporting columns: the secret police, the state bureaucracy, and the Party, with all three coordinated by the old dictator's personal secretariat. This was perhaps the low point in the Party's career since the seizure of power. Weakened and demoralized by the purges, it became less and less the instrument of social revolution. Decline in zeal, dogmatic stagnation, and bureaucratization were the familiar consequences.

During the fourth phase, which began with several years of instability within the Kremlin, but can still be associated with the name of Khrushchev, there occurred a gradual lessening of the conflict between society and the regime coupled with a certain maturation—and social acceptance—of the new order. This phase was made possible by the Stalinist liquidation of all nonpolitically directed social groups, so that the regime could afford the luxury of diminished violence. Thus, Stalinism paved the way for the relative leniency of the post-Stalinist phase. In the political domain, it has been characterized by the re-emergence of the Party apparatus as the dominant political force and by Khrushchev's increasing emphasis on linking technical-economic achievement with broad and intensive ideological indoctrination. The revitalization of the Party and the renewed emphasis on ideology marked an effort to make the system "move again" (to borrow a phrase made popular during an American election), and the personal success of Khrushchev is in large part due to his instinctive perception of the organizational compulsion of the Party toward ideology-action. Stagnant in Stalin's later days, the Party almost naturally responded to a man whose appeal involved a reactivization of the Party's historical role.

THE PARTY AND THE IDEOLOGY

Obviously, Khrushchev's political system is not the same as Stalin's, even though both may be generally described as totalitarian. Therefore, the next step in examining the nature of the Soviet system in 1961 is to find clues to important continuities and changes by looking more closely at certain key dynamic aspects of its political regime. The most revealing seem to be the role of the Party, the role of ideology, and the role of violence. Each of these will be considered briefly, and certain issues involved will be highlighted.

Perhaps the most important single development of the last few years in Soviet politics has been the revitalization of the Party and the reassertion of its dominant position in Soviet life. One by one, the secret police, the state administration, and the army, as well as the planners, the intelligentsia, and the youth learned this lesson—sometimes painfully. A direct relationship between the leadership and the masses has thus been reasserted—the relationship of access and mobilization.[2]

But the implications of this may be even broader. The recent assertion of the Party's role suggests that certain conclusions reached by sociologists concerning the comparative roles of specialized experts and managers in large-scale American enterprises may be highly relevant to the Soviet totalitarian system. These studies have implied that experts are unable to provide the "integration" that a large-scale, diversified organization requires, since such integration is often incompatible with the narrower, highly specialized focus of the expert and requires a high degree of skill in human relations, which an expert rarely possesses. Studies of the two groups have further suggested the following important differences between them: personality types, background and promotion procedures, orientations and goals.[3]

It would not be far-fetched to suggest that the role of manager in the Soviet system, if that system as a whole is viewed as a goal-oriented large enterprise, is performed by the *apparatchiki* of the Party. They are the ones who are skilled in human relations or in social organization, who have a sufficiently wide perspective to provide broad integration, and who rise from the bottom with their minds and skills focused on the over-all objective of the organization—the fulfillment of its historical purpose. Thus, they enjoy an inherent advantage over the expert, whether he is a technocrat or a professional bureaucrat. This picture is confirmed by the valuable studies of Soviet political and managerial elites carried out in recent years by Armstrong and Granick.

A certain amount of technical expertise does not handicap a manager. In fact, it makes him more able to cope with his sometimes recalcitrant experts. The same holds true with the Party. The growing penetration of its ranks with technically and professionally trained individuals need not mean a transformation of its organizational values or a decline in its vitality. A local Party secretary who can now deal with a recalcitrant expert by both cajoling and arguing with him may be far more effective in asserting his goals than his predecessor of twenty-five years ago, who probably approached the problem with loud swearing and ignorant threats. What is essential, however, is that this political goal-orientation of the Party be maintained. The recent intensification of indoctrination within the Party suggests that the leadership intends to maintain it. The vital importance of *propagit* activity and the size of its staffs on all levels are good indications of the importance attached to this task by the regime. Technical know-how and doctrinal sophistication was the secret of the Jesuits' success. It is important and revealing to note the CPSU's efforts in this direction.

In a consideration of the changing role of the Party, it is also revealing to examine the problem of leadership conflicts within it. The character of the contestants, the issues over which they fought, and the methods used to resolve the struggles cast light on both continuities and changes within the Party and the system. In this connection, it is instructive to ask who, what about, and how? For example, take the difference between some of the major Party opponents of Stalin and Khrushchev. Trotsky symbolized the revolutionary, almost anarchistic traditions of Communism. To defeat him, Stalin skillfully exploited the instinct of self-preservation of the Party, not ready to sacrifice itself on the altar of world revolution. No contrast could be sharper than between that flaming and flamboyant revolutionary and the quiet dullness of Malenkov, a Party *apparatchik* who, perhaps in spite of himself, became the symbol and maybe even the spokesman of the managerial technocracy. Similarly, when the time came for Stalin to move forward with domestic reforms, he was opposed by the brilliant and articulate Bukharin. Is it just a coincidence that his counterpart thirty years later was the hulking, sullen, and anything but effervescent Kaganovich? The change that has taken place within the top elite is well symbolized by the individuals who failed in the struggle for power—and this change is as important for the future as any of the similarities that one may wish to draw between the victors.

The issues of the conflicts are also revealing. They no longer involve basic questions of the very survival of the Communist regime. The problem now is how to promote a venture that has been eminently successful but cannot stand still (much like a prospering business in a competitive environment). Domestically, the major challenge to the ruler's power does not come from the visionaries and revolutionaries. To succeed, a challenger must be able to work within the ruling organization, and this successful organization, even while compulsively requiring ideology-action, does not wish to undertake reckless initiatives. The greater threat comes from the dogmatic conservatives and the undogmatic managerial and technical intelligentsia. To the former, all the necessary wisdom of theory and practice is to be found in the experience of the years 1928–53. To the latter, the construction of socialism tends to be equated with the process of building a technically advanced industrial society—and once the process is completed, the wherewithal for the further operation of society can come from within the technical cadres of experts and specialists.

But to each group, the other is a greater threat than Khrushchev's leadership, and hence the two neutralize each other, much the way the Left and Right did in Stalin's early days. At the same time, they both illustrate the fact that the ruling party is no longer faced by fundamental questions of life and death, that the revolutionary phase of the great dilemmas of principle and practice is finished.

The "how" of the conflicts, however, serves as a timely warning against premature conclusions concerning any fundamental change in the internal political practices of the Party. In both cases, the victorious contestants were individuals who skillfully combined their perception of the innate collective interest of the ruling elite with effective manipulation of the Party's *apparat,* particularly through the secretariat. It would be difficult to explain Khrushchev's success merely in terms of his control of the secretariat. After all, his opponents were strong in it as well. The case was similar, as Deutscher shows in his *Prophet Unarmed,* with respect to Stalin versus Trotsky. Both involved muted appeals for support and perceptive appreciation of the dominant aspirations of the ruling elite. And in both cases, there were inherent pressures toward centralization of power in the hands of a single individual, pressures that he could exploit but which he alone could not have generated. Considering Khrushchev's age, one is well justified in analyzing clues to a new—or at least potential—struggle for succession, and in doing so one can learn a great deal not only about the power struggle itself but also about the *Gestalt* of the ruling party.

A discussion of the role of the Party as a dynamic factor in Soviet politics leads directly to a consideration of the political function of ideology. (See Chapter 4 for a discussion of how ideology affects the external conduct of Soviet leaders.) One of the most distinctive features of the Soviet system, and particularly of its ruling regime, is its conscious purposefulness. Everything it does—in fact, its very existence—is related to a conscious striving toward an announced but not exactly defined goal. Since this action is necessarily focused on the immediate tasks facing the Party—be it collectivization and class struggle at one time or the further limitation of the individual's opportunity for personal ownership at another—varying emphases of the ideology are involved in such actions. These provide clues to the changing preoccupations of the regime. As already noted, much of the ideological emphasis today is centered on making Russia a highly advanced, technically skilled nation, and the Party a rational, efficiency-oriented organization. But it is one thing for the Party to be rational in its operations and another matter if this rationality begins to impinge on the utopian ends of political action and instead makes the efficient functioning of the system an end in itself. It is the Party and the ideology together that provide the system with its built-in momentum. The decline of either would force the regime to rely almost exclusively on terror, as did Stalin, or face the prospect of far-reaching transformation of the system.

Therefore, internal indoctrination within the Party is of prime necessity. It is important that power within the Party should not gravitate into the hands of "experts," but that broad, purposeful "generalizers" remain at the helm, assisted on the one hand by loyal Party experts (Gosplanners, or managers) and on the other by the watchdogs of ideological purity. The split between these extremes is more objective than subjective. Both are subjectively loyal and dedicated, but with the modernization and development of Soviet society the Party, as noted, has necessarily absorbed the new, highly trained elite, with the concomitant danger of gradual change of orientation within its ranks.

Partly as a balance, and partly almost by a process of reaction, there has developed within the Party a professional cadre of "ideologues," a group of specialists in doctrinal matters, who bear little resemblance to the creative revolutionaries of the 1920's. Yet, the growth of the *agitprop,* and its professionalization, is in itself an indication of the process of change that, in this case, involves strenuous efforts to maintain the commitment of the Party membership to the Party ideology and to express that commitment in action.

At the risk of excessively speculative generalization, one may perhaps suggest the following scheme as far as the present relationship between the Party members and the ideology is concerned: The very top of the Party hierarchy is generally staffed by "ideology-action generalizers," individuals like Khrushchev, Aristov, and Kozlov, with the extremes of technical experts (who may be said to specialize in aspects of action alone) and of ideologues (who specialize in ideology) both represented. It would appear that among the probable successors to Khrushchev the ideology-action generalizers still predominate. (Of the various individuals one may mention—Kozlov, Polyansky, Brezhnev, Aristov, or Suslov—only the last one is an ideologue, and none is a narrow expert of the Kosygin type.)* On the intermediary level, there are two broad categories: the professional Party bureaucrats, the *apparatchiki,* from among whom the top level generalizers eventually emerge, but to whom, on the whole, the ideology has become internalized and is not a matter of continuous preoccupation; and secondly, the large staffs of the *agitprop,* containing the often dogmatic, doctrinaire, and conservative professional ideologues. They are the ones who most often view any new departure as a betrayal. In the lower echelons, it is more a matter of simple stereotypes and formulas than fanatical commitment, although some cases of the latter can be observed even by a casual visitor to the U.S.S.R.

* It may be tentatively posited that the ideology-action generalizers at the apex are usually in a closer relationship to the ideologues than to the more subordinate experts. On lower levels, the Party *apparatchiki* are usually in a closer relationship to *agitprop* than to the experts. (By closer relationship is meant less direct subordination of the latter by the former). In revolutionary times (in early post-1917 Russia or even in China today), there tends to be a relative fusion between the ideology-action generalizers and the ideologues (symbolized by Lenin or Mao Tse-tung). With stability, a process of differentiation has taken place, and in some respects the *apparatchiki* come closer to the experts. In recent years, Khrushchev has been trying to counteract this process by stimulating increased activity by the *agitprop* and by assigning greater responsibility to the *apparat,* thus compensating for the necessarily greater importance of the experts, given Soviet industrial-technical development.

However, it should be remembered that all three levels operate within a system that already reflects institutionally the basic notions of the ideology and that a more assured mood thus prevails than in the period of struggle against the old order.

Another aspect of the role of ideology involves the almost frenetic efforts of the regime to indoctrinate the masses. It is not an exaggeration to say that indoctrination has replaced terror as the most distinctive feature of the relationship of the regime to society, and perhaps even of the system itself as compared to others. With the completion of the destruction of organized intermediary groups between the regime and the people, with the basic outlines of the new society erected, the emphasis on class struggle has given way to a massively organized effort to instill in the Soviet people the values of the ruling party. The closer one studies the Soviet political system, the more one becomes impressed by the totality of the effort and the energy and resources committed to it. There is just no comparable example elsewhere to this total effort (in the words of *Pravda,* September 14, 1960) "to rear the new man." While the Party often meets with major difficulties because of boredom, hostility toward uniformity, absence of free contacts with the West, and disbelief and/or just formal acquiescence, it is able to exploit a very major advantage—that it is in a position to link the process of ideological indoctrination with technical modernization of society, which has become the universally accepted good in our age. It is not an accident that, in all recent discussions of propaganda, the Party has been stressing the need to link the two, and because of its monopoly of power the Party can make modernization seem like the consequence of its ideologically inspired action. The organizational compulsion of the Party for ideology-action thus becomes the source and the means of modernization, thereby strengthening the Party's social legitimization.

Thus, ideology has the important effect of transforming the Party's power into authority and of replacing terror as the chief buttress for the Party's power. This is a major change from Stalin's days. It is now clear that terror has to be seen as a manifestation of a particular stage in the development of the system. In its most intense form, terror manifests itself during the break-through stage of totalitarianism, when the old order is being destroyed and the new erected. At that stage, the secret police emerge as the crucial organ of the regime, dominating the political scene. Given the objective of total reconstruction, terror quickly pervades the entire society, and the police become supreme. To the extent that the dictator is inclined toward a personal appreciation of violence, in some respects such terror can be even more extreme and sadistic. However, it is doubtful that the social impact of Soviet terror in the 1930's would have been much less even if Stalin had not enjoyed (as it is alleged he did) the physical liquidation of his enemies and friends. As terror mounts, the apparatus of violence becomes institutionalized and develops a vested interest in the continuation of the operation. Therefore, it is difficult to halt it rapidly, while the ruling elite is naturally aware of the storehouse of social hostility accumulated by terror and becomes fearful that abandoning terror might bring about a violent upheaval.

Terror thus tends to perpetuate itself even after the regime's need for it recedes.

The abandonment of terror was facilitated by the involvement of the terror machine in the struggle for succession after Stalin's death. While it is likely that terror would have declined anyway, the desperate need to decapitate the secret police, lest it decapitate the various heirs-apparent, precipitated a more rapid decline of the secret police than perhaps would have been the case. It is quite conceivable that Stalin's successors were pleasantly surprised to find that their system could work and work quite well, or even better, without terror and that the social response was not one of a revolution but of gratitude. Thus, they pushed the process forward, and today one may justifiedly say that terror is no longer a dominant feature of the system. To be sure, the potential is there, and it acts as a restraining force. But it no longer pervades society, and it is certainly no longer one of the central means for effecting social change.

Instead, organized coercion performs the function of enforcing societal conformity. The acceptance of the new forms of society by a large part of at least the urban population permits the regime to utilize social orthodoxy for the purpose of enforcing ideologically desirable behavior. The Comrades' Courts and the Citizens' Militia, staffed by narrow-minded and intolerant low-level activists, are forms of organized mass coercion designed to stifle politically dangerous individualism that might threaten the pattern of positive indoctrination. For that purpose, the potential of political terror in the background and organized social intolerance in the forefront is sufficient. A volun-

tarist totalitarianism can be far more effective than a
terrorist one.

The theme running through the three aspects previously discussed is the organizational compulsion of the
Party toward enforcing social integration around its overt,
stated, dogmatic beliefs. To abandon these efforts to ide-
ologize society, even if this process is already highly ritu-
alized and may no longer involve general individual
commitment, would signal the first real step in the direction of the transformation of the system. The regime has
shown that it can rule with far less violent means than
was the case with Stalinism, but the kind of power it needs
to continue changing society, even if at a decreasing pace,
demands a degree of social integration that can be achieved
only if a sense of purpose, organizationally expressed, is
energetically maintained.* Only then can the emergence
of alternative values be avoided; only then can the appearance of groups showing alternative goals be prevented; and
only then can the individual be faced with the politically
paralyzing dilemma of the one alternative—that to be
against the regime is to be *against* everything and *for*
nothing.

POLITICS AND SOCIAL DEVELOPMENT

In recent years, a great deal has been said about the
social-economic development of Soviet society. It has been
argued that the achievement of the highly literate and eco-

* One might add that an older example of the expression of the
survival instinct of a goal-oriented movement through such organizational
compulsion toward indoctrination and social integration is provided by
church history.

nomically mature society would necessarily cause a profound transformation of the political order, and in this connection the words "liberalization" or "democratization" have often been used. The burden of the preceding pages suggests that politics is still supreme within the Soviet system, although such political supremacy cannot be viewed as existing in a vacuum, independent of the social-economic context. The role of the dynamic factors in shaping Soviet politics clearly must be seen within a framework relating them to the significant changes that have taken place in the U.S.S.R. over the last few decades, and this has been taken into consideration in the preceding discussion.

There can be no doubt that several aspects of Soviet society have particular relevance to a discussion of the Soviet political system and pose special problems for it. The relationship between the regime and four such sectors—agriculture, the industrial organization, the intelligentsia, and the evolving public organizations—deserves special note.

For the past few years, agriculture has been in the forefront of domestic policy dilemmas. The failure of Stalinist policies to improve agricultural production appreciably forced the succession leadership to re-examine some hitherto sacred tenets concerning the untouchability of the Machine Tractor Stations and to adopt urgent measures to expand the acreage of arable land, to improve productivity, to increase individual incentives for the deplorably underpaid *kolkhozniks,* and (last but not least) to strengthen the direct control of the countryside by the Party. The extremity of the crisis, as well as the fluid

83

situation in the leadership, quickly led to the emergence of alternative positions, and the Central Committee plenums that attempted to deal with the situation (starting with the September, 1953, plenum and including both the 1958 and the 1959 meetings) also became arenas of bitter political conflict, with consequent political casualties at the very top. However, what is particularly interesting in terms of a political system that is ideology-action–oriented is that, although ample evidence has been cited even by the Soviet leaders (as well as by the recent statistical yearbook) showing that productivity on private plots far outdistances the "socialist sector," all the solutions offered, both the conservative and neo-Stalinist as well as the innovating Khrushchevist ones, specifically excluded any alternative that could increase agricultural production at the cost of the ideology. Furthermore, the least controversial measures have been those resulting in highly successful steps to politicize fully for the first time the agricultural sector. The present trend, involving the amalgamation of collective farms, their increasing formation into state farms, and the liquidation of private plots and livestock, suggests that efforts to improve production and the lot of the collective farmer by making him, in essence, similar to an industrial one, involve conscious political direction based on ideological considerations. In effect, the way of life of roughly 50 per cent of the Soviet population is still being actively and profoundly changed by political action.

The situation in the industrial sector is somewhat different. Here, too, the question of reforms was linked with serious political conflict, as was openly admitted after the

July, 1957, plenum, particularly at the December, 1958, plenum. However, neither the policy issues nor the measures actually taken involved, to the same extent at least, the problem of ideology versus efficiency or further politically directed changes in the way of life of the urban proletariat. Instead, the issues centered on the problem of planning and managerial organization and on their relationship to effective Party control. The solution adopted—namely, the system of *sovnarkhozy*—is familiar. In many individual cases, it certainly involved important changes in the accustomed mode of life. A bureaucrat's family, moving from Moscow to Irkutsk, may perhaps have reflected, in the course of the long train ride on the Siberian railway, on the relationship of political decisions to their way of life. However, a more significant consequence of the reforms was that increased efficiency of operations (achieved, it is claimed, by de-bureaucratization and decentralization) was linked to a consolidation of direct Party control over the industrial sector. The Party remained as the only vertical and horizontal source of social and political cohesion in Soviet society, and on all levels of the industrial organization direct Party participation in the decision-making process was assured. A Party secretary, Brezhnev, personally supervised the reorganization, and it is the responsibility of republican and regional Party secretaries to make certain that increasingly frequent manifestations of *mestnichestvo** are subordinated to over-all national objectives as set by the top leadership.

The relationship with the intelligentsia is more difficult

* Overemphasis of local considerations; literally "localism."

85

to define. As a group, it enjoys special privileges, and many of its members have direct access to the leadership circles. As a result, it can make its influence felt perhaps even to a disproportionate degree. Furthermore, the experience of recent years, particularly of 1956–57, shows that there is restlessness and even dissatisfaction among a great many Soviet students, writers, and poets. The intellectuals in particular have always been the carriers and the disseminators of new ideas, either indigenously conceived or adopted from abroad. However, in order to do this on a politically significant scale, they must live in an environment that is at least passively receptive.* By and large, one is forced to conclude that those intellectuals who are inclined to question the existing taboos have not found the Soviet Union to be either actively or passively receptive. With the possible exception of the small artistic communities in Moscow and Leningrad (within which a novel like *The Trial Begins* could be created), the regime has so far been able to prevent the development of anything like the intellectuals' clubs of Warsaw or Budapest, and it has successfully maintained its general monopoly on all means of communication.† Furthermore, the first generation of urban dwellers of the U.S.S.R. is

---

* An actively receptive community is one that, because of a continuous and often competitive interplay of groups, is necessarily responsive to the impact of new ideas; New York and Paris are good metropolitan examples. By a passively receptive society is meant one that does not set up purposeful impediments to the inflow of new ideas.

† The political experience of intellectual unrest in Hungary and Poland on the one hand and in China on the other might be relevant here. In the former, it was closely associated with demoralization in the Party and led to an eruption. In the latter, it did not penetrate the Party, and the regime was able to suppress it quickly.

not the epitome of intellectual tolerance, and the regime successfully appealed in 1956–57 to the anti-intellectual bias of the masses when it needed to intimidate the intellectuals. Beyond that, Party control over *nomenklatura*, publications, rewards, and awards has served to contain occasional individual violations of the politically determined limits.

As far as the intelligentsia as a whole is concerned, the prevalent tendency seems to be toward professionalization and a compartmentalization of interests. An engineer or doctor is given relatively unlimited opportunities for advancement on the basis of merit, provided he meets certain minimum political criteria. Party membership, but not necessarily an active one, is often a necessary condition for a position of major professional responsibility, but as long as formal behavior lives up to the political norm and the expected degree of ideological know-how is demonstrated, the regime does not impose heavy and objectionable demands. To the extent that such a relationship can be appraised, it would appear that there is at present mutual satisfaction with this arrangement.

A relatively new phenomenon in the regime-society relationship is the emphasis placed on the public organizations that are to absorb certain state functions in view of the latter's gradual "withering away" in the course of the transition to Communism. Although as yet little of major significance has passed into the hands of such organizations, there appear to be three major objectives for stressing them: to revitalize public zeal and stimulate interest in the transition to Communism; to develop through popular participation a form of citizens' control over bureaucratic operations; and to enforce societal conformity over wayward behavior. All three suggest that the regime is increasingly confident that it enjoys some measure of popular support and that, if it is to increase the scope of social initiative, it will do so at the bottom, where ideological intolerance and social conformity are probably the strongest. At the same time, the regime will be in a better position to appraise popular moods (recent Soviet interest in public opinion polls is revealing) and will therefore be better informed for the difficult task of both running and changing a large and an at least semi-modern society.

The Soviet political system thus involves one-party dictatorship, with its outstanding characteristic being the active indoctrination of the society in the Party's ideology and the shaping of all social relations according to that ideology. For this reason, words such as "liber-alization" and "democratization" are somewhat mislead-ing. They are, after all, terms used to describe a process of political, social, and economic change that took place in Western societies under entirely different conditions— essentially organically, often spontaneously, and usually pluralistically.

The process of change within a totalitarian society has to be seen in a perspective that considers the means used to modernize the existing society, since the means that have been used tend to affect the longer-range patterns of development. In the Soviet Union, a primitive society was industrialized and relatively modernized through total social mobilization effected by violent, terroristic means wielded by a highly disciplined and motivated political elite. The very nature of this process is inimical to the emergence of a separate managerial class (not to speak of the even more amorphous concept of "a middle class"), which would be a first step in the direction of a limitation of the Party's power. Furthermore, a society developed under total political direction has a need for continued political integration on a national scale, since the liquidation of both the private economic sector and all informal leadership groups creates a vacuum that must be filled. In such conditions, the Party—its discipline, morale, and zeal—remains the determinant of change.

To the extent that this ruling party desires to maintain continued mobilization of society, it may even be argued that a modern industrial society provides that party with more sophisticated tools of social control and permits it to maintain that mobilization. Indeed, one may further state that the more modern and developed the society, the more malleable it is. Terror and violence may be necessary to change a primitive, uneducated, and traditional society rapidly. Persuasion, indoctrination, and social control can work more effectively in relatively developed societies. Czechoslovakia, in contrast with Poland and Hungary, would be a good example. Close students of Soviet scientific development have already noted that there are ominous indications that even more sophisticated techniques of psychological and social manipulation are in the offing. Gide's observation has not yet reached its stage of obsolescence.

The present Soviet discussions of what the future Communist society will be like offers us a revealing picture that should not be ignored (if past experience is a guide). Professor S. G. Strumilin, the Soviet expert on the transition to Communism, assures us (in *Novy Mir,* July, 1960) that: "Any Soviet citizen who enters the world will automatically be enrolled in a nursery, transferring to an established children's home and then, according to age, placed in a boarding school. His transition to productive life or to further special studies will also be arranged." The Professor adds: "Too much parental love often has catastrophic results for the children, hindering the development of the children. We are absolutely opposed to the old tradition that regarded children as the 'property' of the parents." People will live together in large communes, eating together; their children will play only with communal toys: "personal property, such as toys, ice skates, bicycles, will not be recognized in the commune. All gifts received by the children will go into the 'common pot' and be there for everybody." Everyone will be dedicated, behavior will be enforced by the sheer weight of communal orthodoxy, which necessarily excludes individual self-assertion. Dachas and automobiles will no longer be the objects to be desired by an individual, and public servants will toil with a dedication deeply rooted in the Communist ideology.

It may be comforting to dismiss all this as sheer fantasy, but to the extent that the stability of the present regime depends on the continuous, even if gradual, implementation of the ideology into practice, such descriptions are a good guide to an understanding of the goals of a party ruling an increasingly mature and voluntarist totalitarian system. They suggest that the CPSU has not yet resigned itself to playing merely the role of a Soviet chamber of commerce. Indeed, every indication points to the conclusion that Soviet society is again on the eve of momentous changes whose process of execution is not likely to weaken the Party's power.

THE IMPACT OF EXTERNAL AFFAIRS

It is at this point that a consideration of the interaction between external and domestic affairs becomes particularly relevant. Many past cases of such interaction can be cited. For example: in 1926, the China policy and the domestic struggle for power; in 1936, the mounting war threat and the domestic purges; in 1946, Stalin's conviction of a basic hostility toward the West and the domestic decision again to give the Soviet society a taste of War Communism (radical political and economic policies); in 1956, the general situation in the Soviet bloc and the anti-Stalin campaign. In some ways, however, it could be argued that the relationship is becoming increasingly significant. In the past, Stalin's regime was basically inward-oriented and isolationist, but today the U.S.S.R. is deeply involved both in world politics and in the complex process of running an international Communist empire. On the one hand, this involvement strengthens the role of the ruling party since it seems to demonstrate its claim that it is leading the U.S.S.R. to greatness. At the same time, what happens abroad is now much more relevant to domestic Soviet politics. That is why Kennan's thesis that political containment could lead to a domestic mellowing or breakdown of the Soviet system was at least premature. It assumed a relationship between external affairs and domestic politics that did not exist in Stalin's time. It exists today, however, but in a much different way.

The emerging diversity within the Communist orbit, and the necessary Soviet adjustment to it, means that increasingly the hitherto uniform ideology tends to be expressed and emphasized in different ways. Furthermore, the recent admonitions that war is not inevitable and that a nuclear war would be a universal catastrophe necessarily challenge the conception of an immutable and objective historical process and make a purely subjective and perhaps even an irrational factor—someone's decision to start a war—a deciding issue in the historical process. Both tend to threaten the domestic ideological uniformity of the system either by its penetration by competitive ideas or by the relativization of the ideology in view of its varied interpretations in different Communist states. In either case, there is a danger of the gradual domestic erosion of the absolutist ideological commitment. The officially admitted fear of war, stemming in large part from the objective factor of the destructiveness of nuclear weapons, is closely related to the increasing domestic social desire to enjoy the "good life." In the history of the regime, there has always been a tension between a genuine desire of the regime to improve the lot of society and its fear of doing it too quickly, which would be politically and economically disastrous. With the "victory" of socialism in the U.S.S.R. finally assured, the regime finds itself increasingly able to respond to social pressures for a better life. However, it would be politically very dangerous if both at home and abroad a mood of general social relaxation were to prevail. The sense of dynamism must be preserved. The continuous need for the Party's dictatorship and, therefore, for its ideology-action must be demonstrated.

The present response is a compromise both at home and abroad. It is no longer a matter of violent large-scale social revolution at home, but "the extensive transition to Communism," with its hopes for the good life, does mean that the march forward is being continued. And abroad, it is not a matter of outright violent hostility toward the enemy, since that carries with it the danger of total destruction. Rather, it is again a compromise: peaceful coexistence, but an ideological offensive, translated into the encouragement of radical nationalist revolutions made possible by the peaceful and paralyzing mutual nuclear blackmail of the U.S.S.R. and the United States. Peace with victories will serve to strengthen the Party's claim that history is still unfolding, that it must continue its mission, that there is no fraternization with the enemy —but all without war.

Nevertheless, relativization of the ideology is implicit in such adjustments and carries with it dangerous internal implications. The domestic power of the totalitarian system depends on the commitment to an absolutist ideology. But an ideology that is right only in some places, for some people, and at some times cannot provide that conviction. If the ideology becomes a relative one, it will be deprived of the fanaticism and dogmatic conviction that have provided the momentum for sacrifice, forceful action, and internal unity. History teaches that relativization is the first stage in the erosion of the militancy of any system of dogmatic ideas.

The appearance of diversity within international Communism, a diversity that the Soviet regime initially desired to limit only to the institutional side while retaining ideological uniformity, carries with it the danger that varying ideological emphases may result either in splits or in the development of a silent agreement to disagree. This is a novel situation for a movement that has matured in the belief that ideological unity and organizational unity are absolutely essential. It also suggests that if such gradual erosion is to take place and if, in its wake, the Soviet political system is to change fundamentally, the change will have to come primarily from the outside and not from the inside. Originating in bona fide Communist states and formulated within the framework of the common ideology, alternative and more tolerant notions might gradually penetrate the ruling elite and only afterward affect the society as a whole.* However, if one considers what and how long it took for foreign ideas to penetrate the far less controlled Czarist Russia, to merge with domestic trends, and eventually to emerge supreme, and if one weighs all this against the internal power of the Communist regime, one may well be justified in cautioning that this erosion should be awaited with a great deal of patience.

---

* There might be an analogy here to the political history of religiously oriented societies. It was only after the Protestant and Catholic states learned to coexist with one another and, for that matter, with non-Christian states that Protestants, Catholics, and others learned to live with one another *within* given states. An "interfaith council" in the United States is thus not only an example of conscious toleration but also of a decline in absolutist commitment.

Part II

FOREIGN AFFAIRS

4. Communist Ideology and International Affairs

My purpose here is to discuss briefly the nature of the Soviet ideology, its impact on the Soviet approach to international affairs, and the prospects for ideological erosion.

THE NATURE OF THE IDEOLOGY

A reformist social doctrine ceases to be an intellectual abstraction and becomes an active social agent, or an ideology, when it is applied to concrete situations and becomes a guide to action. No doctrine, however elaborate or sophisticated, can provide answers and guidelines to fit all aspects of historical development. The shaping of events necessarily involves situations that are either unforeseen or dictate a logic of their own, even if initially fitting the theoretical assumptions. Doctrine is then "creatively" extended, new principles are extrapolated from the original set of assumptions, new generalizations crystallize,

97

and, finally, the identity of the ideology emerges. Ideology is, in effect, the link between theory and action. (See the Introduction for a working definition.)

The persisting and important role of ideological assumptions in the thinking and actions of Soviet leaders (which, it is argued here, is essential to an understanding of their conduct) can be appreciated only if it is seen in a perspective that takes into consideration the various factors that go into the shaping of an ideology. The triumphant assertions that the Soviet leaders are abandoning their Marxism or Communism, voiced in the West with such monotonous regularity and persistent ignorance,* might possibly be dismissed more quickly if the usual image of an abstract and arid Marxist dogma were to give way to a better appreciation of the inextricably close linkage between the Soviet social environment and the Soviet ideology. It is precisely because the ideology is both a set of conscious assumptions and purposes and part of the total historical, social, and personal background of the Soviet leaders that it is so pervading and so important.

Without undertaking a comprehensive review of the development and substance of Soviet Communist ideology, it may be useful to recall in "capsule" form some of the

---

* To cite just a few such assertions: Stalin has returned to true Russian nationalism (he was not even a Russian); Soviet Russia is interested in Czarist territorial ambitions only; Stalin is a skillful practitioner of power, but is not interested in ideology; Malenkov is essentially a spokesman of pragmatic managers; Khrushchev is a level-headed experimenter; Mikoyan is really no different from our businessmen; the Soviet Union is accepting incentives and efficiency and is chucking "doctrinaire" Communism.

factors that have gone into molding it (or perverting it, as the purists would claim), thereby making it much more a part of the Russian reality and infusing it with genuine social vitality. Such variables as the general historical context, the role of personalities, the manner in which a foreign doctrine was understood and absorbed,[1] the emergence of the Party and its special organizational experience, and finally, the process of shaping a new society—all interacted dynamically to give the ideology its particular flavor and emphasis. No one of these factors alone can be said to have determined the character of the Soviet ideology; taken together, they do help us to understand how it emerged and developed. In summary form, the following assumptions and principles may be said to be part of the ideological framework within which the Soviet leaders evaluate and organize their perception of the outside world: Marxist doctrine is the basic source of their commitment to economic and dialectical determinism in history, and of their persistent conviction that the vehicle of history is the class struggle. (These themes were often reflected by Mr. Khrushchev in his little homilies on American television.[2]) Closely related to this "scientific" conception of history is the apocalyptic image of the future and the belief in the inevitable triumph for their form of social organization. The basic organizational principles that they apply to society are rooted in the conviction that most social evils are derived from private ownership; under certain circumstances, even an inefficient public or state ownership is to be preferred to private ownership. (Countless examples of this basic prejudice are available from past and present Soviet experience, as well as from Eastern Europe and China.)

The experience of the Bolshevik leaders in pre- and post-Revolutionary Russia resulted in the emergence of a series of further basic postulates, which together with the above categories constitute the Soviet ideological framework. Probably the most important of these is the Soviet conviction that the construction of socialism anywhere requires that power be wielded solely by the Communist Party. This belief, in part rooted in the Russian experience and in part reflecting the institutionalized vested interest of the ruling elite, has become a fundamental thesis of the Soviet leaders. Its impact on their vision of the world should not be underestimated, for it colors particularly their appreciation of changes occurring in the underdeveloped parts of the world. Similarly, the Leninist concepts of the seizure of power, with their emphasis on violent revolution, went far in the direction of establishing the supremacy of "conciousness" over "spontaneity" in historical processes, in turn consolidating the importance of the organized and conscious agent of history. The Soviet commitment to monolithic dictatorship and intensified class struggle as necessary attributes of the socialist construction thus again reflects the combination of doctrine and practice becoming ideology. Similarly, Lenin's discussion of the nature of imperialism reflected his pragmatic awareness that theory must always be related to a given reality; in the case of his historical era, it was to provide a meaningful insight into the inner dynamics of the underdeveloped and restless part of the world. The Marxist approach was the basis for the Leninist theory of imperialism and gave Lenin his point of departure as well as his basic analytical tools. However, the combination of Marxist doctrine, Russian revolutionary experience, social-economic backwardness, and the vested interest of the ruling Bolshevik Party resulted in the notion that social developments throughout the world operate on the basis of a sharply definable dichotomy—a dichotomy that is proof per se of an unbridgeable hostility between the emerging socialist state (later a system of socialist states) and the rest of the world.[3] A paranoiac image of the world conspiring against socialism easily followed.

All these conceptual and analytical factors combined serve to organize the Soviet vision of international affairs, to define goals, and to evaluate reality. These aspects should not be confused with the utopian elements of the ideology, which are necessary as part of a long-range vision and which perform essentially a rationalizing and legitimizing function. Confusing these two, or failing to distinguish between Marxist theory and the ideology, can lead to the simplistic conclusion that Soviet ideology is merely a cynical sham, consciously manipulated by the Soviet leaders. Similarly, it can result in the opposite and extreme conclusion that the Soviet approach to reality can be understood merely by consulting a Marxist handbook. I have already tried to show that the Soviet Communist ideology must be viewed as combining certain doctrinal assumptions with principles derived from the theory but closely reflecting the specific reality of those who subscribe to the ideology. It then becomes part of the reality and an autonomously existing factor, conditioning behavior through the selection of the various policy alternatives that may exist at any particular moment.

Its Role and Impact in International Affairs

How, then, does the Soviet Communist ideology affect the Soviet approach to international affairs?[4] Here, a distinction must be drawn between short-range and long-range prospects. The former are naturally much more often determined by the imperatives of the moment. For example, on the matter of choice of international friends, Soviet freedom of action was severely circumscribed in June, 1941, quite unlike the situation in the summer of 1939. In the latter case, the essentially ideologically determined conclusion that the objective of the West was to embroil the U.S.S.R. in a war with Germany dictated a policy of creating the conditions for conflict among the capitalist powers—that is, giving the Germans the freedom of action they considered necessary for the commencement of hostilities.* However, Soviet short-range moves are only in part a function of the situation as created by outside forces. They are also the consequence of certain long-range commitments made by the Soviet Union itself, and in that sense they are the product of the factors that shape the nature of that long-range com-

---

* A strong case could be made that Soviet behavior in the fall of 1938 had the same objective. Soviet aid to Czechoslovakia was conditioned on France moving first; if war had broken out, it is quite possible that the U.S.S.R. would then have used the Polish and Rumanian refusal to let Soviet troops through as an excuse to stay on the sidelines. In the meantime, the conflict between the capitalist powers would have been precipitated.

mitment. From that standpoint, they do feel the impact of ideology on Soviet external behavior and policy.*

The general Soviet approach to international affairs is strongly affected by the fundamental Soviet assumption that all material reality changes continuously through the clash of antagonistic contradictions. This conflict is said to be the basic law of social development until such time as socialism becomes a world system. As a result, the Soviet approach to international affairs is characterized by an intense preoccupation with change. This awareness of continuing change, and the conviction that the inner nature of that change is understood only by them, creates the basis for the faith of the Soviet leaders that they have unraveled the internal logic of history and that their policies are not merely an aspiration but a "scientific" calculation.

The preoccupation with change results in a continuing concern with the question: At what point do quantitative changes become qualitative? Communists have not always been successful in answering it, but there is at least a persistent awareness among them of the problem. The following sequence of questions is usually examined by the Communists when defining their policy: What is the nature of the present historical phase? What is the meaning of the relationships prevailing between economic forces and political institutions? What direction are they taking? Who is our major enemy? Is the enemy subjective

---

* For instance, the Marshall Plan may be seen as a consequence of certain ideologically influenced moves by the Soviet Union in 1946–47. However, it created immediate problems to which the Soviets had to respond and about which they had relatively little choice.

or objective? (For instance, Japan at one time was "subjectively" hostile in its policy while "objectively" a progressive force since its industrialization was subverting the feudal order.) Who are our allies, subjectively and/or objectively? At what point will we part with our allies? What ought to be the pace of our efforts to stimulate further change?

At almost every important turning point in Communist policy, such questions have come to the forefront and have often resulted in heated debates and conflicts. But once understanding and evaluation have been achieved, the debate ceases and the policy is set. Understanding, evaluation, action—these are the stages of policy formulation. Such was the case, for example, with the concept of the people's democracy in Eastern Europe in the years 1945–47. Applied to specific instances, ideology thus defines first of all the ultimate purposes to which policy must aspire. In that sense, it has remained basically unchanged throughout Communist history. Second, to the Soviets it makes possible the understanding and evaluating of various historical phases that serve as stages on the way to the final goal. In policy-making, these phases are not so broad as the general Marxist historical stages (e.g., feudalism or capitalism). Rather, they identify the basic character of the specific phase within the present epoch—as, for instance, a revolutionary phase, a quiescent phase, a phase dominated by aggressive imperialism, or a phase in which the essential force changing history is "the liberation struggle of the colonial peoples." Once properly understood, the nature of a particular phase reveals who the main enemy is and what measures ought to be adopted.

Preoccupation with proper "phasing" reflects a distinctive kind of continuous and conscious effort to identify, dissect, and reconstruct reality. Ideology thus infuses Soviet foreign policy with a keen appreciation of the close relationship between international affairs and domestic developments. Rejecting the conception that international affairs involve principally the interplay of various nation-states attempting to promote their national objectives, the Soviets view the world as a continuing struggle among a variety of interests—domestic, social, economic, political, as well as national. The interplay between nation-states is merely one, and often only a formal, aspect of international affairs. In the Soviet view, for true understanding, one must seek to establish the correlation of the various forces that are dynamically coexisting within a given society and chart their likely pattern of behavior as well as their likely influence in the future. For instance, much of the recent Soviet foreign policy toward the United States appears to be based on the calculation that forces at work within American society are bent on achieving a modus vivendi with the U.S.S.R. and are willing to pay a relatively high price for it.[5]

The preoccupation with change, the willingness to adjust to the particular "historical" phase, and the quest to understand the inner dynamics of other societies has not, however, prevented the ideology from infusing Soviet foreign policy with a sense of continuity in purpose. This sense of continuity is derived from the militant conception of relations, in which reality is viewed as being a continuing conflict. In the Soviet view, occasional equilibriums result in international *détentes;* they do not, however, halt the fundamental process of change and therefore cannot create enduring conditions of stability. This means that any political arrangement is binding only until it ceases to interpret accurately that reality. For this reason, no long-range commitments to the status quo can be contemplated except in terms of communicating with those who are accustomed to thinking in terms of the present and who regard the changing reality as part of a vaguely definable, free-flowing, and gradual historical process. Given that, the over-all purpose of Soviet foreign policy is to remain associated with, and to stimulate, the evolution of these processes of change in the direction of ultimate consummation. The ideological commitment inherent in this attitude permits the Soviet leaders to remain persistent in their task, transcending reversals and failures that inevitably occur and despite shifts in their own policies.[6]

An absolute certitude of self-righteousness is also an inherent aspect of the ideological influence. Compromises and adjustments can never be ends in themselves and are only accepted by the Soviet leaders if they appear to be warranted in terms of their pursuit of higher ends. While in practice this may appear to differ little from the attitude of those nations that view such compromises in a favorable light and are prepared to consider them as ends of policy, the significant factor is the built-in element of transiency involved in any such compromise as far as the Soviet leaders are concerned. Indeed, Soviet policymakers face a continuing dilemma of having always to differentiate between tactical expediency and concession of principle in order to be able to make such compromises.* This difficulty, however, is minimized by the Soviet conviction that, in the final analysis, Soviet foreign policy is always objectively correct since it is geared to history. From this it follows that, since war is a violation of the basic pattern of historical development (i.e., an effort to stop or reverse history), the Soviet Union is always for peace, even at a time when waging war. The capitalist concept of peace being essentially static, and therefore antiprogressive, is objectively against peace.[7]

In addition, despite the shifts and turns in Soviet foreign policy in the last several decades, a persisting attribute of its long perspective is the sense of compulsive obligation to assist the spread of Communism throughout the world. This universality of goal makes Soviet foreign policy something altogether different from Czarist foreign policy or, for that matter, from the relatively vague and rather generalized American desire to see a "free" but otherwise undefined world. (However, there are some striking parallels between the Soviet view and the tradi-

---

* Khrushchev alluded to this difficulty in a speech on October 31, 1959:

> But one must not confuse mutual concessions in the interest of peaceful coexistence with the concessions of principle, in matters that concern the actual nature of our socialist system, or ideology. In this there cannot be any question of concessions or any adaptation. If there are concessions of principles, in questions of ideology, it will mean an incline toward the position of our foes. It will mean a qualitative change in policy. It will be a betrayal of the cause of the working class. Whoever adopts such a course will take the course of betraying the cause of socialism, and, of course, the fire of merciless criticism must be opened upon him.

107

tional American image of America as an active symbol of certain universal norms.) Admittedly, Soviet foreign policy, especially in its short-term aspects, is concerned with national security, frontiers, national power, etc.[8]—factors that inherently introduce similarities with Russia's traditional concerns.[9] Quite unlike their predecessors, however, the Soviet leaders view these issues in terms of certain long-range perspectives and not as ends in themselves. Indeed, the Soviet conception of their own security is inherently offensive; as long as alternative political systems exist, there is continued need to be preoccupied with security issues.[10] Because they see themselves as part of a historical process toward a defined end, the Soviet leaders are compelled to view any effort to "stabilize" or to "normalize" the international situation as a hostile design.[11]

The universality-of-goals aspect of Soviet foreign policy also makes it clear that, while the concept of "national interest" may not be irrelevant to an understanding of Communist foreign policy, to be useful it must be linked to the ultimate ideological objective. As far as Communist leaders are concerned, Soviet national interest is that which increases the power and the capability of the U.S.S.R. to promote Communism. Communist ideology, therefore, does not raise the dilemma of national versus international objectives—at least, it did not until such time as a series of other Communist states came into being. Dovetailing of national and international interests is hence another important ideological element and permits the Soviet leaders to strengthen their power without power becoming the sheer end of their actions. Ideology that makes power both a tool and an end allows the Soviet leaders to be continuously concerned with the maximization of their power but without that power becoming an impediment to the fulfillment of ideological values.

For instance, even if the reason for enforcing dramatic and, indeed, revolutionary changes in Eastern Europe were merely the desire to strengthen Soviet power over the area and not to construct Communism per se, the mere fact that the method of strengthening that power was conceived in terms of large-scale social and economic changes showed the underlying ideological bias. One can certainly argue that a more moderate program would have created much less resistance and hence would have favorably affected the Communist power situation. The standard Communist answer—Communism is not safe without creating a social upheaval that uproots the existing interest groups—in itself reveals an approach to problems of political power that is strongly tinged with ideological assumptions. Similarly, in economics, the issue of collectivization is a case in point. Also, as far as the international Communist movement is concerned, ideology permits the Soviet Union to enjoy an additional operational advantage without always having the actual power to control the behavior of the various Communist parties throughout the world. Ideology, as a binding system of belief, thereby translates itself into a factor of power.

Admittedly, the ideological factor can and often does create difficulties. It can lead to excessive dogmatic evaluation of the situation, stimulate premature optimism, or simply mislead.* Furthermore, as far as the Soviet leaders are consciously aware of the ideology's role as a unifying bond for international Communism, it may tend to limit their freedom of action lest this unity be strained. This consideration was less important during Stalin's days than before and after the dictator's rule.

However, on balance, the various roles of the ideology cannot be viewed merely as a liability. There is a tendency in the West to view ideology as something irrational and to counterpoise it against pragmatism and empiricism.

---

* The strict application of Marxist theory to an examination of world affairs occasionally leads the Soviet leaders to make some extraordinary mistakes, such as their belief in the revolutionary Marxist nature of the world proletariat. The Russians were bitterly disillusioned to discover that the working classes of Germany and the East European countries were by no means either solidly pro-Soviet or the source of power they expected.

See R. S. Tarn, "Continuity in Russian Foreign Policy," *International Journal*, 1950; reprinted in R. A. Goldwin (ed.), *Readings in Russian Foreign Policy* (London: Oxford University Press, 1959), pp. 689-705:

Another important miscalculation stemming from the application of Marxist theory has been the Soviet belief in the inevitability of American economic depression after the war, and the belief that because of the contradictions in capitalism the two principal capitalist powers, the United Kingdom and the United States, would soon fall out. The appreciation in the Kremlin of Marshall aid was also based on the belief that the United States must acquire new markets in Europe in order to postpone the coming depression in the United States. Even as regards colonial theories they have had a difficult task in reconciling the peaceful handing over of power by Britain in India and Burma—though Indo-China and Indonesia have provided plentiful ammunition for the Soviet theorists. Finally, a supreme miscalculation has been the failure to gauge properly the continuing force of nationalism, particularly in Eastern Europe.

Other examples might be the Soviet policy in China, both in the 1920's and the mid-1940's; in Yugoslavia in 1947-58; and in Eastern Europe in general in 1956-57.

Ideology and International Affairs

From what has already been said, it would appear that ideology is not incompatible with rational behavior, once the basic assumptions are granted. While these assumptions may or may not be rational, they are at least so far removed from immediate concerns that they do not produce a conflict between the ideology and a rational approach to reality. The goal of an ultimate world-wide Communist society, allegedly determined by history, may be irrational, but it does not necessarily impose irrational conduct.

Secondly, and perhaps more significant, some of the concepts of the ideology do offer meaningful insights into international affairs. The preoccupation with the nature of the domestic dynamics of other societies and the realization that economic processes create political problems that are international can result in a more meaningful appreciation of reality than arguments about traditional national goals or moralistic pontifications to the effect that democracies are inherently peaceful and more powerful, while dictatorships are warlike and ultimately doomed. For all its limitations, Soviet ideology at least seems to point to some of the inner mechanisms of international affairs. The approach of Western statesmen is still often derived from an image of international affairs shaped by the emergence of nation-states. As long as these states operated in an environment in which mass emotionalism, particularly nationalism, was not politically determinant, international politics could function relatively stably on the basis of certain commonly accepted rules.[12] The intervention of mass public opinion, rallying around first nationalist symbols and then ideological ones (democratic or totalitarian), necessarily transforms interstate political conflicts into national ones, with profound social-economic overtones. The difference between the Vienna Congress of 1815 and the Versailles Treaty of 1919 are symptomatic.

The Soviet Communist ideology has made an important contribution toward the transformation of international politics from a "game" with certain commonly accepted rules into a profoundly intense conflict, insoluble without a major social transformation either of some of the participating societies or at least of the outlook of some of their elites. However, given the fact that modernization, particularly industrialization, has produced a world-wide awakening of the political consciousness of the masses, the Communist ideology, even while serving to intensify conflicts, underscored the necessity to base international conduct less and less on legal and diplomatic devices and more and more on political-sociological insights that cut across state frontiers. The Communist realization, even though often not successfully exploited in policy, that the key to the future of our era lies in the transformation of the colonial and underdeveloped parts of the world preceded similar recognition on the part of Western chancellories by several decades. The focusing on certain long-range social-economic and political trends, a matter increasingly accepted in the West since World War II, has doubtless contributed to a more sophisticated appreciation of certain international issues than efforts to operate international affairs on the somewhat artificial plane of legal-diplomatic interaction between nation-states increasingly charged with blinding emotional content.

For the time being, that same ideology distorts its own insight by viewing international affairs through a perspective that sees them as operating on the basis of a hostile dichotomy between two rigidly, abstractly, and simplistically conceived social-economic systems. The Soviet Communist ideology, even while consciously grappling with certain social problems, introduces into international affairs an element of profound instability and conflict by rejecting the notion that social-economic change might be *unconsciously* taking place in all societies faced with certain similar difficulties, thereby reducing the degree of their diversity. Soviet insistence (derived from the conceptual elements of ideology already noted and from their general impact on Soviet foreign policy) that ultimate peace depends on the total victory of a particular social system led by a particular political party injects into international affairs an element of a fundamental struggle for survival not conducive to conflict resolution.

PROSPECTS OF IDEOLOGICAL EROSION

There is a difference between ideological change and ideological erosion, although the two are closely related. Change has to take place if ideology is to continue to respond to social needs. However, when the ideology begins to lose its social vitality, either by becoming so dogmatic that it no longer corresponds to reality or because reality has so changed that even the widest stretching of the ideology can no longer encompass it, the change develops into erosion. The ideology becomes merely declamatory or simply fades away. These verbal

113

dialectics can perhaps be made meaningful by a discussion of the impact on the ideological framework that shapes the Soviet foreign policy of the following three sets of factors: (1) the interaction of Communist objectives and domestic change; (2) the emergence of the Communist bloc; and (3) the impact of international affairs.

Communist objectives and social change. The development of the Soviet ideology has been closely linked with the various phases of the activity of the political movement that embodies the ideology and, beyond that, with the various men who have stood at the helm of that movement. A recent and perceptive analysis of these stages characterized them as that of transplantation, adaptation, and implementation.[13] To the extent that it is possible to compartmentalize social development into neat phases, the first two may be said to have been closely associated with the name of Lenin, and the third with Stalin. Each of these phases was dominated by some central objective that necessarily magnified or minimized some of the ideological principles to which the movement subscribed. For instance, the emergence of the Party as the central, indispensable agent of history has been a crucial ideological ingredient of the entire span of Soviec development, a necessity interdependent with the changing central objective. On the other hand, the stage of transplantation permitted or maybe even required a measure of internal dialogue that gradually became incompatible with the subsequent stages of adaptation and implementation and with the character of the movement that such a dialogue bred. Increasingly, the antiauthoritarian and democratic

elements of the doctrine gave way to ideologically supported discipline, ending finally with the physical liquidation of all those who by their mere presence reminded
the Party or its leader of the movement's former diversity.
Similarly, the essentially antistate orientation of the early
revolutionaries gradually gave way to the acceptance and
then to the enshrinement of the state as a central and
positive factor in effecting the desired socio-economic
change. The building of a new industrial society also
meant that the principle of egalitarianism had to be aban-
doned and be replaced by a highly stratified social system.[14] The emphasis on a mounting class struggle during
the difficult phase of implementation again reflected both
the dynamics of the central objective and the impatient
disposition of the Party leadership that came to power
in that particular phase. Finally, even after the seizure
of power the Party continued to view itself as a conspiratorial movement, and this also helped to define the
character of its relations with the society subject to it
and with the world at large.

The process of shaping new principles or changing old
ones is not without its tensions. One could almost say
that there is a kind of "dialectical" relationship between
an ideologically oriented party and reality. The ideological party attempts to change reality and, in this way, is a
revolutionary force; the new, changed reality for a while
corresponds to the ideology even while gradually changing itself; in time, the ideology may become a conservative
force; a new adjustment is eventually forced, and the
ideology may then again become a revolutionary force.

The varying stages of Soviet Communist ideology—Lenin-ism, Stalinism, Khrushchevism—and the relatively violent transitions from one to the other can be seen as part of this dialectical relationship between ideology and reality. Yet, it is exactly this adaptability that permits the ideology to exercise a continuing influence and prevents it from becoming sterile and irrelevant, thereby allowing it to retain a certain identity of its own.

However, in the present period two factors threaten to translate this process of change into erosion. The rais-ing of the banner of Communist construction, proclaimed by the Twenty-first CPSU Congress in an effort to revital-ize the ideological sense of purpose, will produce much sooner than hitherto might have been expected a con-frontation between reality and ideology. This confronta-tion might threaten the role of the Party as the agent of history and undermine the validity of the ideology. As long as the Party was actively shaping Soviet society and as long as that society was mere putty in the hands of the leaders of the Party, the position of the Party could not be contested. But a highly industrialized Soviet society, in-creasingly conscious of its achievements, could cease to be a passive object and could begin to exert pressures even on the Party. These pressures now seem to be most timid, but so are the initial stirrings of life. Even most restrained social pressures—as, for instance, those in favor of a higher rate of consumption or more freedom in the literary arts—would augur a changing relationship and, as a result, a somewhat changing conception of the ideology. Some alert Communists, more alert perhaps than

Khrushchev, have already signaled warnings that excessive emphasis on industrial indexes and on material well-being as the expression of the achievement of socialism-Communism could result in the unconscious acceptance of many "bourgeois" values by the Communists themselves.[15]

In the meantime, with the passage of years and with the changed social conditions, the very factors that shaped Marxism into Soviet-Communist ideology—the specific historical conditions, the personal background of the Bolshevik revolutionaries, and the manner in which they perceived their Marxism, the dynamics of the movement and its early experience, or, in other words, the objective and subjective factors that shaped the ideology—will have receded into the past. (To a freshman class entering a Soviet university in 1961, Stalin is already a historical figure.) The impact on the ideology of a policy designed to achieve material well-being for a society that has already gone through the most difficult phase of industrialization is bound to differ from the impact of a policy of violent industrialization applied to a backward society. Both the objective and its context are different. What might then happen to the ideology?

A delicate hint of this dilemma is revealed to us by Khrushchev's efforts to return to Leninism. Compared even to Stalin, Khrushchev is a crude thinker whose ideological views are more a matter of a series of preconceptions than a conscious search for relevant formulations, as was still the case with Stalin. But even Khrushchev came to feel that somehow the Stalinist ideology and the Stalinist movement got out of tune with reality. His emphasis on Leninism represents an effort to return to something that seems to evoke a positive echo in the Soviet society of his day. He hopes in this way to recapture the old spirit of the ideology. But little does he realize that these positive echoes are evoked by elements that were "lags" even from the pre-Leninist phase and that Leninism was increasingly combatting: internal democracy, dialogue, doctrinal discussions, not autocracy, dogma, and ideological dictation. None of these need threaten the basic Marxist postulates concerning the nature of reality, to which both the ruling movement and Soviet society could continue to subscribe. However, even a gradual and unconscious return to the original doctrinal assumptions would involve an eventual erosion of the ideological trappings and, with it, of the dogmatic perspectives on world affairs.

The impact of the Communist bloc. In the initial phase of its existence, the Communist bloc served to strengthen the ideological conviction that history is on the side of Communism (or vice versa). The expansion of Communism to include one-third of the globe, effected by force of arms or by revolution, seemed to recapture some of the old revolutionary fervor that had been denied the Russian Communists since the 1920's. History was again in its dynamic phase. To this day, the Soviet leaders glory in the size and population of the camp and frequently cite these as proof that "the east wind is now blowing over the west wind." Furthermore, as long as Stalin lived, the expansion of the camp did not raise insurmountable ideological difficulties. Even the old theory of capitalist encirclement was still maintained, to be attacked, finally, only as late as 1958.* However, this dismissal of capitalist encirclement did not involve an important ideological reconsideration; rather, it was a matter of reassessing the relationship of forces in the international arena and reaching a more optimistic (and as it happens, a more correct) conclusion.

As far as new Communist-ruled states were concerned, after a brief transition period, they adopted an essentially Stalinist pattern of domestic restructuring and conceptions. The Soviet experience in "construction of socialism" was adjudged to have universal validity, and consequently a complex of methods and beliefs, which formed the Soviet ideology and reflected the Soviet adaptation of Marxism, was grafted onto all the ruling Communist elites, whatever their intellectual and political heritage. Stalin's death soon revealed the inadequacy and the fundamental instability of this application. And the subsequent search for new forms of ideological and political unity within the camp underscored the full complexity of the problem of applying Soviet ideology, with its universal aspirations, to varied national conditions.[16]

Without retracing the involved series of attempted solutions and without discussing their relative merits, it can be observed that the efforts to develop common ideological prescriptions for the post-Stalin Soviet bloc came face to

---

* Addressing the Twenty-first Party Congress on January 27, 1959, Khrushchev stated: "The situation in the world has fundamentally changed. Capitalist encirclement of our country no longer exists." On August 15, 1951, *Bolshevik*, reaffirming that capitalist encirclement still exists, stated the following: "Capitalist encirclement is a political term. Comrade Stalin has stated that capitalist encirclement cannot be considered a geographic notion."

face with two obvious and related difficulties: the matter of different social contexts within which an ideology matures and the problem of varying stages of "socialist" development. The first of these could be ignored as long as Stalinist power and Stalinist prestige were available and could be applied so as to universalize the Soviet outlook. Furthermore, the early stage of Communist rule in the newly subject nations meant that the main thrust of Communist efforts was directed at consolidating their power and at destroying the old society. These essentially negative tasks did not raise ideological problems as acute as the later one of building new social institutions.

However, Stalin's death and the dissipation of Stalinism took place when the attention of the Communist leaders was increasingly turning to the latter objective. Within the context of relative relaxation, faced with domestic problems peculiar to their own societies, some of them increasingly eschewed Soviet solutions and step by step began to feel the full weight of their own social traditions and their own "apperception" of the ideology. A general consequence of this was the emerging ideological diversity that characterized the bloc in 1956–57 and potentially exists even today, despite conscious and essentially expedience-motivated efforts by the ruling elites to re-establish ideological uniformity.*

Moreover, the varying stages of social-economic development of the various countries within the Soviet bloc inherently produced different problems requiring different solutions. China, going through an economic and

* The high point of these efforts was the November, 1957, conference of the ruling Communist parties and its declaration.

social revolution at a pace even more rapid than the
Soviet Union did in the most violent Stalinist phase,*
could not escape drawing primarily on those aspects of
the ideology that justified the application of violence,
maximized the power of the Party, simplified international issues into simple relations of hostile dichotomy,
and viewed with profound suspicion any voices of modera-
tion.[17] The Soviet Union—on the brink, if not of a Communist fulfillment, then at least of reaping a partial
harvest of several decades of social sacrifice—was becoming
increasingly concerned with rationalizing the operations
both of its own society and of the bloc. Many Communists
in Poland, Hungary, and Rumania, countries suffering
the pangs of transition from a rural society to an industrial one and lacking the indigenous support that both
the Russian and Chinese Communists enjoyed, were increasingly coming under the influence of "revisionism"—
that is, abandoning the simplifications of the Soviet ideological outlook, increasingly viewing the problems of social
transformation as organic worldwide processes, requiring
also a gradual and continuous transformation of social consciousness. On the other hand, the leaders of industrially
advanced East Germany and Czechoslovakia, not faced
by social-economic tribulations, were increasingly sympathetic to the Chinese outlook, since it provided the
political justification for their politically unstable regimes.
Striking evidence of this was provided by the Chinese
tenth-anniversary celebration in Peking in October, 1959:
On foreign-policy issues and on Chinese domestic policies,

* This can be readily seen from comparative data on economic development, for instance, for analogous periods of their "socialist" development.

including the "Great Leap Forward" and the communes, the East Germans and the Czechs adopted the most enthusiastic line, quite in contrast to the Poles and the Russians.

The consequence of this differentiated ideological conditioning, of the different stages of development of the respective socialist states, as well as of different interests of the ruling elites, has been an occasional diversity of outlook on a variety of important issues. In the case of China and the Soviet Union, this diversity seems to involve an issue not new to the Soviet Communists: To what extent can a Marxist revolutionary cooperate with the existing social forces and merge himself with the observable trends in the direction of the inevitable victory? To what degree must he remain alienated from the world, rejected, and strive to alter it by first destroying it? Perhaps it would not be too gross an oversimplification to say that the crux of the problem was whether peaceful coexistence with the enemy was transitionally possible. There are interesting historical precedents for questions such as these. At one time, Mensheviks believed that the historical stage had arrived when they could face the forces of reaction on their own ground and that victory was within their reach. As Haimson has stated it:

Absolutism stood already on the brink of extinction. . . . Plekhanov no longer had any serious reason to be concerned over the preservation of orthodoxy in social democracy. . . . Axelrod no longer had much cause to worry over the task of organizing forces capable of overthrowing absolutism; and Martov could look forward confidently

to a moment in the not-too-distant future when the power
of the hostile forces reigning in the world would at least
be significantly reduced.[18]

The Bolsheviks rejected such views, feeling that Menshevik policy could only dull the sharp edge of the
revolutionary trend and allow the enemy to create the
preconditions for even more durable, albeit more subtle,
oppression. In some ways, however, the Soviets could be
viewed today by the Chinese as adopting an essentially
Menshevik position in international affairs. Overconfident
of their strength, they seem to overlook the danger that
premature optimism can only lead to a demobilization of
revolutionary zeal. And, conversely, the Soviets might
well feel that the Chinese overlook the decisive, objective
fact of the contemporary phase of international affairs—
that of Soviet power, which allows the Communist bloc
to adopt the policies of coexistence from positions of
strength.[19] Nevertheless, the presence of a more *revolutionary* state in the camp cannot help but be disconcerting
to the Soviet claim of ideological "virtue" and must
certainly cause ideological uneasiness in the Soviet ranks.
Indeed, it is this capacity to adopt more radical policies
than the Soviet Union that is the major source of Chinese
ideological leverage within the camp.

Quite a different challenge to ideological unity is
raised by some of the East European Communist states.
The most extensive statement of contemporary East
European revisionism is contained in the program adopted
by the Yugoslav Communist party in April, 1959.[20] The
general response of the camp to it has been to anathematize

the Yugoslavs. But within all the ruling European Communist parties, such views are entertained by many members, particularly among the intellectuals, and provide the underpinning for potential ideological disunity.[21] The reason for this is simply that the Soviet ideology will not meaningfully reflect or shape reality in the Eastern European context unless Soviet force is available to back it. Anyone familiar with the ideological traditions of Polish left-wing socialism, with the cultural climate of the country and its "political style," or with the role played by the populist writers in Hungary in the shaping of Hungarian radicalism would agree that forceful measures would be necessary to prevent the dilution and revision of Marxism-Leninism when that ideology comes to be embodied by large mass movements within these countries. Such forceful measures were undertaken by the small, dedicated Marxist-Leninist minorities existing in these countries, but even they found it difficult to remain immune to their environment. Much the same could be said for some of the other Communist-ruled states.

It was this environmental influence that was at the root of the 1956 crisis, and the same consideration has recently forced the Soviet leaders to equivocate on the old issue of the class struggle after the seizure of power. In response to the needs of Soviet society and attempting to explain the "aberrations of Stalinism," Khrushchev negated and condemned the principle of the mounting class struggle as a Stalinist distortion of Marxism-Leninism. In 1959, however, faced in Eastern Europe with the dilemma of social opposition to socialist construction and fearful that his abandonment of this Stalinist principle might strengthen the hands of the revisionists there, he modified it "dialectically":

> The Twentieth Congress of our Party rightly criticized Joseph Stalin's mistaken proposition that the class struggle grows sharper with progress in socialist construction. But criticism of this proposition certainly does not mean that we can deny the inevitability of class struggle in the period of socialist construction. . . . This development does not proceed along a straight line. Class struggle in the epoch of building socialism can intensify at certain periods in connection with some of the changes in the internal and external situation and assume an extremely sharp form, up to and including the armed clash, as was the case in Hungary in 1956.[22]

Khrushchev's efforts were symbolic of the growing necessity to adjust the ideology to varying national conditions. In spite of his efforts, however, the radically different conditions that the ruling Communist elites encountered in Eastern Europe as compared to Russia in 1917 or to China in 1949 pose a continuing dilemma to the unity of Communist practice and, therefore, to the unity of the ideology.

Despite Soviet efforts to maintain an ideological equilibrium, the consequence of this growing diversity, and the Soviet elasticity in response to it, is to *relativize* the meaning of the ideology. For forty years, the Soviet leaders have been accustomed to rejecting those who talk a different "language" than they and to ejecting those who use the same language to disagree. Now, for the first time, they have to tolerate fellow Communists who use similar concepts to reach different conclusions. Even today, one should increasingly speak not of Communist ideology but of Soviet Communist ideology, Chinese Communist ideology, Yugoslav Communist ideology, etc. And since it was the Marxist-Leninist ideology's claim to universality that originally stimulated such intense Soviet involvement not only in the domination of its neighbors but particularly in directing the character of their domestic transformation, the increasing diversity in ideological emphases threatens the universal validity of even the Soviet ideology itself and thereby undermines one of the factors that shape the Soviet approach to the world. It also threatens the domestic legitimacy of this Soviet ideology by denying its central claim—that is, its universal validity—which is used as a justification for its domestic application. Efforts to reassert unity in response to this threat can further divorce the ideology from reality, while the toleration and resulting extension of such diversity threatens to introduce elements of relativism dangerous to the cohesion of the ideology.

This vicious circle also brings up the problem of the relationship of the Soviet Union to international Communism. In the immediate post-Revolutionary phase, the new Soviet leaders were quite prepared to sacrifice what traditionally has been considered Russian national interest in order to promote the spread of the revolution. They were thus willing to sanction Polish independence and to cede territory in the hope of stimulating a revolutionary chain reaction.[23] The failure and disappointments experienced in the 1920's resulted in the convenient merger of ideology and national interest, and the defense and expansion of the revolutionary base, Russia, became synonymous with the interests of Communism. The same applied to international Communists in their relations with the U.S.S.R. The emergence of several Communist states could challenge this identification, despite continuous efforts to assert Soviet primacy and confluence of interests. After forty years, even a marriage of convenience can develop a measure of stability, and certainly the social pressures within the highly nationalistic U.S.S.R. would oppose policies designed to promote international Communism at the expense of the U.S.S.R. One may even assume that Soviet leaders would think automatically that any policy harmful to the Soviet Union would harm international Communism and would oppose efforts to transform their "universal insight" into a mere parochial perspective. Yet, it is not too much to assert that differing viewpoints could crystallize in Warsaw or Peking, or even, for that matter, in East Berlin. The divorce of Communist ideology from Soviet national interest would not strengthen the ideology within the U.S.S.R., while their continued linkage is likely to breed resentment and weaken that ideology elsewhere.

The impact of international affairs on ideology. After the seizure of power, the Soviet leaders had to adjust to an international reality that did not quite fit their earlier expectations. The adjustment was not easy and involved a series of conflicts between reality and ideology (e.g., the controversy generated by the Brest-Litovsk negotiations with Germany). Even after their power had been consolidated, the spread of the revolution was both expected and artificially stimulated by Moscow. Gradually and painfully, however, ideology began to correspond to reality, and the principle of "socialism in one country" emerged.[24] It took a long time for this principle to lapse, and many Soviet actions after the war with respect to their new Communist neighbors were rooted in this principle lagging behind the new political situation.

As far as Soviet conduct in the international arena was concerned, given the weakness of the new Soviet state, ideology could not exercise a wide latitude in action. The number of policy alternatives open to the Soviet Union was relatively limited, if one excludes political suicide as an alternative; and Communist ideology, unlike the Nazi one, lays the greatest emphasis on self-preservation. Faced with international politics that operated essentially on the balance-of-power principle, the Soviet Union, in order to pursue its ideological objectives, had no choice but to attempt "to play the game," employing the openings that the game provided to its best advantage.* In summing up his evaluation of the role of ideology in Soviet foreign policy, Moore correctly concluded that, as far as the Soviets were concerned, "the choice of antagonists or allies has been determined not primarily by ideological factors, but by the structure of the balance of power system itself." [25]

The situation has changed with growing Soviet power and with the even more rapidly growing Soviet sense of confidence. For the first time since the 1920's, the Soviet leaders seem to feel again that the day of their victory

---

* Symbolic of this was the acceptance, after some reservations, of the Western diplomatic techniques, rituals, and protocol trappings.

is not far away.[26] However, balancing this are also several factors related to international affairs that eventually could serve to modify this Soviet sense of ideological fulfillment. These may be treated under three headings: stability in Western society, patterns of development in the underdeveloped societies, and the nature of modern weapons systems. With respect to the first, it would appear that in 1947 the Soviet leadership still entertained some hopes that revolutionary upheavals might take place in France, Italy, and/or Greece, and they were counting on the expansion of Communism into Western Europe. Failure of these attempts, followed by a remarkable West European recovery, seems to have convinced the Soviet leaders that in the foreseeable future they cannot count on the duplication of either the Leninist (seizure of power) or the Stalinist (military occupation) form of Communist development. Beyond that, they increasingly appear to be willing to concede that in such stable, prosperous, and democratic societies, an altogether different form of transition from the bourgeois stage to the socialist stage must be contemplated. Khrushchev finally articulated this when he stated at the Twentieth Party Congress that, Lenin to the contrary, a peaceful takeover by the Communist Party was possible and that parliamentary devices could be used to that end. Such a conception comes dangerously close to an abandonment of Leninism, and the Soviet leaders were not unaware of it. Therefore, they refrained from taking the next step (taken by the Yugoslavs)—that of conceding that socialism may be built by social-democratic parties—and they continued to insist that only the

129

Communist Party could effect such a true transition. Nevertheless, the importance of the change should not be underestimated. The change does involve an important modification of their outlook.

The relevance of this change, furthermore, is not limited only to the West; similar considerations could apply in the East, although the Soviet leaders consider it much less likely (Kerala may be an example). It is, however, not the theory of the peaceful transition to socialism per se that poses a threat to Soviet ideology in the East. Rather, it is the related matter of the general method of building socialism. In Soviet thinking the following is required in order to build socialism:

> . . . the leadership of the masses of the working people by the working class, the core of which is the Marxist-Leninist Party, in bringing about a proletarian revolution in one form or another and establishing one form or another of the dictatorship of the proletariat; alliance of the working class with the bulk of the peasantry and other strata of the working people; the abolition of capitalist ownership and the establishment of public ownership of the basic means of production; gradual socialist reorganization of agriculture; planned development of the national economy with the aim of building socialism and Communism, raising the working peoples' standard of living; the accomplishment of a socialist revolution in the sphere of ideology and culture and the creation of a numerous intelligentsia devoted to the working class, the working people, and the cause of socialism; the elimination of national oppression and the establishment of

equality and fraternal friendship among peoples; defense of the achievements of socialism against encroachments by external and internal enemies; solidarity of the working class of a given country with the working class of other countries—proletarian internationalism.[27]

The end result is to be a centrally planned, nonexploitative society with a relatively high standard of living. The Soviets are convinced, given their dichotomic image of the world divided into socialism and capitalism, that only through socialism can industrialization be achieved and a prosperous society constructed.

The new and still underdeveloped states therefore pose the challenge of claiming by and large to be building societies of a socialist type and of actually doing it through democratic political means and highly pragmatic and certainly not Soviet (nor capitalist) economic methods. If they should succeed, and they possibly might with both Soviet ("socialist") and American ("capitalist") aid, the consequence will have to be a major redefinition of the processes of social-economic change, whatever the Soviet ideologues may choose to call the new society.[28] Such a development would strike not only at the ideology and its dichotomic image of social change but even at its doctrinal foundations. It would pose a threat to the entire historical structure of the ideology and would strengthen the appeal of revisionism within the Communist ranks.

The third and probably the most important aspect of international affairs that could promote the erosion of

131

ideology pertains to the weapons systems. The Soviet Union has always considered its strength to be an important determinant of its policy, dictating caution or warranting action. In so far as military strategy is concerned, the Soviet leaders, particularly Stalin, have considered their society to be especially well equipped for lengthy wars of attrition—given its size, morale, endurance, and discipline. That remained the prevailing Soviet doctrine even after World War II, which was not surprising, given the nature of the Soviet experience in it. After Stalin's death, however, following a period of internal strategic debate, the primacy of nuclear weapons in Soviet military thinking was established, with the consequent emphasis on striking power and the element of surprise.[29] As this conception gained the upper hand in Soviet thinking, it was only a matter of time before the converse came to be recognized—that similar strategies might be equally decisive if used by the opponent.

This had immediate bearing on the Soviet thinking concerning the inevitability of war. For a long time, the basic Soviet conception had been that wars were inevitable as long as capitalism, and particularly imperialism, created the economic basis for war. Stalin restated this principle as late as 1952. However, if such a war should occur and if the Soviet Union were drawn into it, there could be only one result: the end of capitalism. Gradually, with the mounting possibility of mutual destruction, the Soviet leaders have been forced to conclude that war is no longer, as Khrushchev put it at the Twentieth Party Congress, "a fatalistic inevitability." The further extension of this shift has involved an increasing willingness to concede that war would be mutually destructive and that it would not benefit either side.[30] The formal explanation for this change in position was that the strength of the socialist bloc, and of the Soviet Union in particular, has become, so to speak, a sufficiently powerful political-military superstructure balancing the economic necessity for war.

Of course, it could be argued that this change reflects increased Soviet confidence that history's scales have finally been tipped in favor of Communism and that rash action, therefore, is to be avoided. In other words, the adjustment is the product not merely of necessity but also of Soviet interest. Furthermore, there can be little doubt that if the military situation were to become one-sidedly favorable to the U.S.S.R., making it invulnerable, the Soviet viewpoint might change again. However, the important point is that, under the impact of the concrete factor of admittedly decisive importance—the problem of survival—the Soviet ideology had to gradually adjust again, modifying a hitherto important ideological assumption. Peaceful coexistence as an alternative to mutual destruction cannot easily be squared with some of the historical inevitabilities inherent in the ideology, even if such peaceful coexistence is defined as competition.* By implication, at least, it does seem to elevate nuclear weapons into a force capable of interfering with history. It would be naïve, of course, to assume that Soviet commitment to such peaceful coexistence is irreversible; but

---

* As if to compensate for this, the Soviet press has recently been stressing the need for intensified ideological struggle against alien concepts and against the capitalist system.

given a general fear of war, the Soviet leaders would have to think twice before restoring "the inevitability of war" principle. However, a necessary precondition for the maintenance of the new formulation is the perpetuation by the West of its destructive capability. Without it, the objective reason for peaceful coexistence will have disappeared.

The cumulative effect of the various processes discussed in the preceding pages could be the gradual erosion of certain ideological aspects of the Soviet perspective on international affairs. The ideological syndrome, containing an oversimplified conception of an antagonistic confrontation between two social systems and of historical change in general, the commitment to conflict, the universality of goals, the sense of self-righteousness, and the belief in the imminence of victory—all could be threatened by the combined impact of domestic change, the emergence of ideological relativism due to the spread of Communism, and the stark threat of nuclear extinction. A growing willingness to accept some common and overt rules of behavior could follow, buttressing the existing informal and undefined restraints on violence that both sides have tacitly recognized. But this process of erosion is at the present time balanced by certain pressures in the opposite direction, which reassert and even revitalize the ideology. The final outcome of these clashing tendencies depends on too many variables to be safely predicted, but uncertainty about the outcome should not obscure the certainty about conflicting pressures.

SOURCES OF IDEOLOGICAL VITALITY

The experience of the German Social Democratic movement with Marxism might serve as a general lesson that one should not expect such an erosion to occur rapidly. It took the German Party a very long time to shed its relatively rigid Marxist orientation, and the final act of liberation from the Marxist doctrine did not take place until its Congress of 1959.* In part, this might be explained by the delaying impact of the Nazi experience and the reaction against the revival of laissez-faire capitalism in Germany. In part, it also reflected the delaying influence of the Party as an organization with a vested interest in its doctrine and of that organization's action commitment, which necessarily stimulated opposition to its Marxism and thereby also intensified belief in it. That this belief was strong and persisted for many years should need no documentation. It does offer, however, a striking illustration of an ideology's capacity to survive even under conditions increasingly remote from those to which the ideology was relevant. It is also to be remembered that this ideology finally began to fade when a democratic political process and democratically accepted changes in socio-economic organization made possible a peaceful re-evaluation of the Party's views and did not pose before it the alternative of disintegration.

In the Soviet Union, several established commitments

* Compare the basic program of Bad Godesberg with the Heidelberg program of 1925.

act as powerful counterforces and protect the ideology from erosion. The most important of these is the institutional commitment in the form of the ruling party. Not much needs to be said about this most important factor. If the ideology were to fade, particularly among the membership, the power of the Party would be threatened, even though ritualization could delay the disintegration. The upper echelons of the Party are very conscious of this. The steps taken by Khrushchev to re-establish the role of the Party in Soviet society and the recent measures adopted to invigorate the ideological indoctrination of the population at large suggest that the Party is determined to maintain ideological consciousness in its ranks. In the foreseeable future, there is little reason to doubt its capacity to do so.

The institutional commitment to ideology is backed by a personal commitment. To individuals like Khrushchev, the ideology is the source of their insight into reality, a conscious treasure to be guarded against pollution (unless by themselves, which is a different problem), the basic course of their education (*Rabfak*, in Khrushchev's case), and the emotional source for their personal sense of life. The present generation of Soviet leaders— men in their early sixties—came of age during the latter stages of the civil war and matured during the NEP and the Stalinist transformation of Russia. Their first contact with the ideology came at a time when the Party was still intensely preoccupied with ideological issues and was attempting—through debate, deviations, and purges—to determine what course to pursue in building a new society. Even a simple young member like

Khrushchev, for example, could not avoid involvement and had to make his choice. Ideology in the 1920's was an important matter, even if one were to focus merely on the power struggles that were taking place. Khrushchev's experience in this period was bound to leave with him a lasting awareness that there is a "correct" and an "erroneous" path and that the Party must always remain conscious of this. In a decade or so from now, and maybe sooner, a new generation of Soviet leaders will come to the fore. The men who are now in their fifties—e.g., Brezhnev and Kozlov—were twenty when Stalin undertook his collectivization drive and defeated all opposition, and they were in their mid-twenties when the Party experienced its great purge. They faced no alternatives. To them, power equaled ideology. The road forward was simple, firmly charted, and not subject to discussion. To such a generation, ideology may be less a matter of conscious preoccupation. This may make them in some ways much more defenseless against unarticulated social processes that quietly erode the ideology. Nevertheless, the habits of thought and the personal experience of the Soviet leaders will act as a braking element on the force stimulating erosion.

Broad social commitment is another "defensive" element. As values become socially ingrained, they resist new values. The reconstruction of Soviet society on the basis of the ideology and the indoctrination of many decades has created a social residue that will resist the intrusion of new ideas, even though the intellectually alert elements may be drawn by them. The influence on the latter can be effective only if they either penetrate

137

the Party or succeed in infusing the society with new notions. Given the nature of the Soviet society, the task for the carriers of new ideas is not easy, unless a major crisis should shake its stability. In some ways, it can even be argued that urbanization and industrialization, achieved within an ideological context and by an ideologically motivated movement, will tend to perpetuate the role of ideology. First, they institutionalize an environment that is based on the ideological aspirations and in time begins to act as a buffer for that ideology; second, through a very tangible sense of achievement, they create a widespread acceptance of the ideology, which, even if lacking its original revolutionary zeal, becomes gradually more pervading; third, the nature of a modern industrial society, which is based on social ownership and has severely limited individual initiative, requires a continuous articulation of societal goals to help preserve the broadly accepted purpose. These factors together are inimical to a rapid erosion of the ideology. Finally, action commitment revitalizes the ideology. Action provokes reaction and breeds hostility and conflict and thereby intensifies belief, steeled by trial. Action crowned by success strengthens the ideology even more. In so far as the masses are concerned, the Soviet leadership has been making strenuous efforts to identify its successes in launching Sputniks or achieving a higher rate of growth with its ideology. Indeed, it may be one of the ironies of the Soviet version of Communism that Soviet military preponderance might become an element that retrenches and intensifies ideological belief.

To the Party membership, Soviet international achieve-

ments are increasingly becoming the "ersatz" method of
establishing the correctness of the ideology, thereby preserving the inner sense of ideological purpose without
which the Party could decay. This ersatz method of
revitalizing the ideology is not entirely a matter of conscious design. Having become a great power, at a rate
certainly not expected in the West and possibly not even
by the Kremlin either, the Soviet Union has a degree
of involvement in the rapidly changing world that by itself tends to create conflicts with other powers. Such
conflicts can easily be translated into ideological terms,
especially as some of the competing units do differ in
values and social systems.

In a sense, therefore, the very act of involvement on
a massive scale—an involvement that in part is also a
function of size and power and would continue to generate
conflicts between the U.S.S.R. and the United States even
without ideology—tends to revitalize the ideology and to
translate even simple issues into broader conflicts. For
instance, one could see the Berlin problem as a proper
matter of international dispute among several parties,
comparable to the Saar. However, quite unlike the Saar
problem, the disputing parties differ sharply in political
and socio-economic conceptions, and any change in the
status of Berlin has immediate implications for the stability of some of the disputing parties. Beyond that, the presence of other Communist states, some possibly more
ideologically radical than the Soviet Union, as well as
the Soviet interest in maintaining unity in the Communist bloc, is likely to intensify the action commitment of
the ideology. The Soviet leaders have recently been mak-

ing strenuous and generally successful efforts to re-establish ideological ties throughout the bloc.

It is these forces that impede the erosion of the ideology and inhibit the Soviet leadership from accepting international affairs as a game with a series of rules; instead, these forces make them insist on treating international affairs as a conflict with only *one* solution. For the moment, possibly the least hazardous conclusion would be to suggest that, while the pressures for the erosion of ideology are gradually building up, the "conservative" forces of the ideology are still well entrenched and have not lost their capacity to exert influence. In the near future, an international "conflict resolution" is unlikely.

5. The Challenge of Change in the Soviet Bloc

The declaration issued by eighty-one Communist parties in Moscow on December 6, 1960, marks a seminal date in the history of international Communism. For the first time in the history of the Soviet bloc, a conference of Communist leaders ended not merely with the usual "unanimous agreement," but also with a silent agreement to disagree. For the first time in about thirty-five years, the general strategy of the Communist parties scattered around the globe is no longer to be set purely in terms of Soviet estimates of what will most benefit the interests of the Soviet Union. Cast aside is Stalin's categorical dictum that "a revolutionary is he who, without arguments, unconditionally, openly and honestly . . . is ready to defend and strengthen the U.S.S.R." What is good for the Soviet Union is no longer automatically also good for the Soviet bloc and for international Communism.

TRANSFORMATION OF THE BLOC

The Moscow conference thus highlights a process of transformation of the Soviet bloc into a Communist one.

This process was inherent in the shift of Soviet power beyond the Soviet frontiers. However, Stalinism, with its insistence on absolute centralization of power in Moscow and on Soviet ideological infallibility, involved a conscious effort to prevent such a transformation. In fact, Stalin did not fear only national Communism—he even rejected its much more subdued variant, "domesticism" (i.e., the effort to make some domestic adjustments while accepting the principle of bloc unity and absolute Soviet leadership).

The Yugoslav break in 1948 was the first signal that an international Communist system could not work effectively merely by applying Stalinist domestic practices to the new Soviet bloc. The change became more rapid after Stalin's death. Several factors prompted it. The new ruling Communist elites in Eastern Europe gradually—and not everywhere at first—became somewhat more confident of their ability to build "socialism," especially if given sufficient leeway to make some domestic adjustments. The presence of an indigenous and independent Communist regime in China "objectively" (as the Marxists would put it) strengthened the case of those within the ruling elites who felt that perhaps Stalinism should be viewed as a transitional phase leading to a more genuine Communist internationalism rather than as an enduring prescription. Another factor prompting change was the accumulated tension of popular, national reaction against Soviet domination—a sentiment that local Communist leaders could not afford wholly to ignore.

In response to these pressures, the post-Stalin Soviet leadership, particularly from the time of Khrushchev's ascendancy, began to search for a new formula for unity of the Soviet bloc. The years 1954–60 can be said to have been dominated by this search. Khrushchev and Bulganin were the first Soviet leaders to visit China, where they sought to warm the frigid relationship created by Stalin's reserve. Later, the Soviet leaders attempted to repair the break with Yugoslavia. They talked of "many ways to socialism." However, the search for unity clearly did not mean that the Soviet leaders were prepared to preside over the dissolution of the bloc. It is evident in retrospect that Khrushchev hoped the bloc could be transformed into a comity of states led by the U.S.S.R. but not terrorized by it. Marxist-Leninist ideology would be the common bond and the source of unanimity.

These efforts were opposed at home and abroad. Some of Khrushchev's colleagues felt that Soviet leadership would be undermined. Others warned that too rapid reform could lead to crises. The vacillations in Soviet policy during this period reflected these conflicting assessments and the sudden pressures of unexpected events. The change in Poland, the eruptions in Hungary, Khrushchev's realization that Tito was not interested in shoring up the Soviet bloc but in sharing in its leadership—all resulted in hesitations and often in retrogressive steps. The secret circular letter in August, 1956, warned the other parties not to follow the Yugoslav path, and after the Polish and Hungarian outbreaks the Soviet leadership began to seek some organizational device to substitute for the Cominform, which had been abolished in 1956 because it was thought to be outmoded.

From 1957 on, the focus of the problem increasingly

shifted eastward. The Chinese leaders shared Khrushchev's desire to create a healthier camp. Just a year earlier, they had encouraged the Soviets to improve their relations with the Poles, even while recommending the suppression of the Hungarian revolution. Subsequently, the Chinese joined Khrushchev in containing Polish diversity, and in November, 1957, they helped Khrushchev obtain Polish recognition of Soviet leadership of the camp. Mao Tse-tung personally insisted that Communist unity required an affirmation of Soviet leadership. Yet, helping to consolidate the bloc did not mean to the Chinese that they should remain silent on the various issues facing it. On the contrary, in the course of helping Khrushchev, they appear to have become convinced that the post-Stalin leadership needed further advice from experienced revolutionaries like themselves. Liu Shao-chi alluded to this in 1960 when he is reported to have stated that Peking had been concerned for some years with the indecisiveness and vacillations of the Soviet regime since Stalin.

SINO-SOVIET RELATIONS

In the fall of 1957, an event occurred that quickly assumed overwhelming importance in the Chinese perspective on world affairs and colored subsequent Sino-Soviet relations. The successful Soviet firing of the ICBM, followed by the launching of Sputnik, was interpreted by the Chinese as signaling a decisive shift in the balance of military power between East and West. The east wind was prevailing, Mao Tse-tung proclaimed. In his view, the Soviet Union now had the means to effect further revolutionary changes in the world, in spite of the militarization of imperialism. But if the means were available in Moscow, the will seemed strangely lacking. The Chinese, therefore, felt duty-bound to infuse international Communism with the will to prevail. Bloc unity was the essential point of departure, but still a means and not an end. Nothing could be done without unity, but unity should not become a substitute for action. Indeed, vigorous action against the common enemy could forge even greater unity than reliance on increased Soviet economic aid to the various Communist regimes or the elimination of the more obtrusive signs of Soviet domination. The almost simultaneous shift in intra-Party politics in China in favor of a more radical wing and the Great Leap Forward provided the domestic underpinnings for these views of the international scene.

The Chinese did not desire war per se, but they were convinced that increased pressure on the West, including that of local wars, was justified and that the West would yield step by step. Furthermore, the Chinese were concerned that fear of war would inevitably lead to the fear of revolution and hence to the extinction of revolutionary zeal in the international movement itself. As a result, they did not hesitate in 1960 to characterize the conception of "a peaceful transition to socialism," propounded by Khrushchev in 1956, as "stupid." They felt that continuous pressure by the militarily superior Soviet bloc would encourage revolutionary upheavals, particularly in the colonial areas. The disintegration of imperialism would soon follow.

The Soviets welcomed the Chinese aid in reconsolidating the bloc. However, in assessing the nature of the present phase of world history, the Soviets tended to see their opportunities in a somewhat different light. Their acquisition of nuclear weapons, and particularly of a delivery capability, forced them to rethink their earlier military assumptions and gave them a greater appreciation of the dangers of mutual annihilation. As a result, the Soviet leaders very carefully abstained from repeating Mao's claim that they had reached a turning point; they have merely reiterated that there is a definite shift in favor of socialism. In their view, the military balance of destructive capabilities is in itself a new and important step forward. It makes possible the encouragement of revolutionary trends in Asia, Africa, and Latin America and the deterrence of Western counteractions in these areas. At the same time, the ICBMs could be exploited politically: In recent years, the Soviet Union has threatened nuclear destruction against its neighbors on at least forty different occasions. In addition, under the protective shield of military power, the Soviet bloc could now bring to bear a new and vitally important factor—its economic strength and technical skill. The combination of mutual military paralysis, political revolutions, and Communist economic power would prevail, without the risk of provoking a desperate reaction from the West.

These basic disagreements were reflected in a host of specific issues. In 1958, China urged a more aggressive attitude in the Middle East crisis and later ignited a new campaign for Taiwan; in 1959–60, there were agitated ideological debates on the significance of the Chinese pattern of revolution as a model for other nations; in 1960,

China showed a distinct lack of enthusiasm for Soviet participation in disarmament talks; during 1958–60, there were growing divergencies concerning revisionism and its implications. Many of these conflicts were veiled in euphemistic terms, but it required no exegesis to recognize their meaning. They were accompanied by a marked decline in Chinese-Soviet cultural exchanges, and there were even hints of some uncertainties on the subject of the Sino-Soviet frontier.

It is obvious that different degrees of alienation and involvement in international affairs, the disparity in stages of economic, social, and revolutionary development, as well as such specific matters as unsatisfied territorial ambitions (e.g., Taiwan) provided the environmental background for such differences. Furthermore, it is very important to realize that the conscious commitments of the two regimes to a jointly shared *Weltanschauung* makes any disagreement between them even more intense. The purposeful effort to define reality and stages of historical change makes consensus more difficult, especially in the absence of a powerful arbiter such as Stalin. In the Communist outlook, general questions of interpretation are usually the points of departure for more specific strategies and tactics. For that reason, it is more difficult in some respects for Communist parties to reach consensus, once they are able to assert their independence, than for Anglo-Saxon nations, whose approach is pragmatic and not so concerned with conceptualization or long-range goals.

At the same time, these disagreements over appropriate strategy and tactics operate within the framework of a larger agreement—namely a mutual method for assessing

147

reality and a common objective. In effect, the common ideology, which defines mutual ends and selects common enemies, and which can be a source of intense friction, also serves to limit the dispute and prevents it from erupting into an open split. In the case of the Sino-Soviet divergencies in 1958–61, it would appear that the dispute was confined by three limits, consciously observed by the parties involved: Both sides have recognized that both would lose by an open split, and hence that unity must be preserved; each realized that the other's leadership is firmly entrenched and that, for better or for worse, Khrushchev would have to deal with Mao Tse-tung and vice versa, a situation quite unlike the one that prevailed in 1948 when Stalin calculated that Tito would fall from power after an open split; the Chinese, for the time being at least, have striven to reassure the Soviets that they are not trying to displace them as leaders of the bloc but are merely anxious to persuade them to adopt a different strategy. The Chinese presumably realized that they could not, at this stage, replace the Soviets as leader since they do not possess the means to enforce such leadership.

The foregoing limits, however, have tended to make the weaker party stronger and the stronger weaker, inasmuch as the partner who is better able to demonstrate overtly his disregard for unity has the advantage of initiative. The burden of responding in kind, thereby further straining unity, or of compromising rested on the more passive of the two. Furthermore, it can be argued that subjectively the Soviet Union stands to lose more by an open split than China, since so much of the international prestige of the Soviet Union and the internal strength of the regime rest on its role as leader of a united bloc of a billion people marching together toward Communism. Indeed, with two partners desiring unity, the one who can appear to be less cautious about preserving it might well gain the upper hand. Thus, in the internal bargaining that has recently gone on between the two parties, the immense military and economic preponderance of the Soviet Union has probably not been decisive. China has been able to persist in her views and even to voice them openly. At the Moscow conference of November-December, 1960, and also at the earlier July session in Bucharest, the Chinese delegation openly assaulted Khrushchev's policies, despite obvious Soviet displeasure.

The Moscow conference, however, was not a Chinese victory. If, in terms of the crucial issues, the statement issued by the eighty-one parties is carefully compared with earlier Soviet and Chinese pronouncements,[1] one finds that by and large the Soviet formulations have prevailed, with some adjustments to meet Chinese objections. It may be surmised that the somewhat greater emphasis on the dangers of war and on the aggressiveness of American imperialism, on the relevance of China to the revolutions in Asia, Latin America, and Africa, on the militant character of national liberation struggles, and the direct condemnation of Yugoslav revisionism all involved adjustment to the Chinese point of view. But on a larger number of issues, the statement bears greater resemblance to earlier Soviet positions. This is so with respect to such matters as: the decisive character of economic development and the role of the "socialist world system" in shaping our age; the destructiveness of war (its horrors were explicitly reiterated); the significance of peaceful coexistence and the possibility of the prevention of war; the importance of the Twentieth and Twenty-first CPSU Congresses and the universal relevance of Soviet experience; the peaceful transition to socialism, the character of "national democracy," and the evils of dogmatism. This impression is corroborated by the unusually frank account of the conference provided by Walter Ulbricht's speech printed in *Neues Deutschland* on December 18. In it, he indicates clearly what the controversial issues were and how the various points were resolved.

There appears to be a twofold reason for the relative Soviet success. The first is rooted in the nature of the Chinese position; the second involves the bargaining process in the meeting itself. Because China is more radically hostile to the outside world, her freedom of action is even more limited, even if initially the Chinese succeeded in putting the Soviet leadership on the defensive. Given their impatience in dealing with the West, the Chinese leaders would probably shrink from actually splitting the Communist bloc, since in their minds the chief beneficiaries of such a split would be the United States and "imperialism" in general. Thus, the range of their bluffing is limited. Furthermore, since their overt support consisted only of the Albanians and a few ot the nonruling parties, a split, or even the threat of a split, could not bring about the desired Chinese objective: a change in the line pursued by international Communism.

The Moscow conference thus had the important effect of articulating a common line for the various parties and of narrowing somewhat the cleavage between the Soviets and the Chinese. Explicit limits to unilateral action by any one party were adopted, and the principle of interference in the internal affairs of member parties for the first time was formally established. Unlike the November, 1957, statement of the twelve ruling parties, which stressed "noninterference in one another's affairs," the 1960 declaration states: "When this or that party raises questions about the activity of another fraternal party, its leadership turns to the leadership of the party in question and, when necessary, meetings and consultations are held." It goes without saying that the principle of interference is likely to benefit the stronger rather than the weaker parties. In his report on the conference, Ulbricht apparently alluded to the Chinese when he stated that "there were objections to the formulation 'general line.' However, if we abandon this principle of 'general line,' vacillations may occur in complicated situations, such as in border problems."

At the same time, the length of the conference and the apparently calculated ambiguity of some parts of the statement suggest clearly that while the Sino-Soviet relationship remains based on common, conscious emphasis on unity, an element of divergence is inherent in the fact that both parties are independent and organizationally distinct. While it is likely that, henceforth, disagreements between them will be more muted and harder to detect, the relationship of divergent unity between them is likely to persist and could easily erupt anew into an open dialogue. The different emphases put on the Moscow statement by subsequent commentaries in *Pravda, Trybuna*

Ludu, and *Neues Deutschland* on the one hand, and in *Hsinhua* and *Zeri I Popullit* on the other, portend continuing dissension.

THE IMPLICATIONS OF CHANGE

The changes that have taken place, and are continuing to take place, within the Communist world have important policy implications for the West. In analyzing these changes, we should abandon the tendency to operate in simple and extreme terms. The bloc is not splitting and is not likely to split. Talk of a Sino-Soviet conflict, of even a war between them, merely illustrates a profound misconception of the essence of the historial phenomenon of Communism, which, while affected by traditional national considerations, has from its very beginning reflected a conscious emphasis on supranational perspectives. Similarly, a change within the Soviet bloc should not be viewed as presaging its disintegration or, conversely, its soon becoming one Communist state. The tendency to see the bloc in terms of such extremes simply obscures the important, if less dramatic, changes within it.

For years, the Soviet bloc was in effect an international system run by one national Communist Party. Today, it is becoming a Communist camp, with the various member regimes participating more actively in the important process of defining the camp's "general line." The events of 1956 served to reassure the Communist chiefs that the West was either unable or unwilling to challenge their domestic power, while the Sino-Soviet "divergent unity" achieved within the bloc meant that opportunities have now been created for more maneuver, without running the risk of expulsion or condemnation as a deviationist.

The last Moscow conference, as well as subsequent events, bear this out. The leaders of the smaller parties— for instance, Gomulka—played a more active role than ever before and have been reliably credited with strongly influencing the Soviet course. Some leaders, like Togliatti, could afford to show their misgivings about the conference by staying away from it. Some of the Latin American representatives offered amendments to the draft of the conference. Others, like the Albanians, could choose to defy the Soviets, even at the risk of incurring the wrath of pro-Soviet parties. It is symptomatic of the new conditions that Ulbricht broke all precedents to accuse the Albanian Party leadership in public and in print, of "sectarianism" and "dogmatism." Yet, both Albania and East Germany remained bona fide members of the bloc. Similarly, on the occasion of the Chinese anniversary, the Chinese sent the Albanians greetings that were both warm and personal —qualities missing from similar messages to Moscow and elsewhere, and notably lacking in Moscow's New Year's message to the Albanians. Similarly, in the course of the recent Albanian Party Congress, the CPSU refrained from greeting Enver Hoxha, while the Chinese heaped praise on the Albanian leader. Still, the Soviet boycott of the Albanian Party chief took place *within* the framework of the camp. The prolonged and successful defiance of the most powerful party by one of the smallest could have infectious consequences, irrespective of the specific issues involved in this case.

Apart from the more overt sympathies of some parties

for Moscow or Peking, there are now pro-Soviet or pro-Chinese factions within most parties. Also, for the first time in the history of the bloc, the various national leaders can quietly exercise options within the bloc itself, rather than having either to choose unity—ergo, subordination—or a split. In effect, the smaller parties can take advantage of the implicit agreement of the two major ones to disagree.

As a result, relations between the Soviet Union and the Communist states and parties vary greatly. In the past, one pattern generally prevailed: close subordination or open hostility (e.g., Yugoslavia). Now there is far greater diversity. In the Soviet-Polish relationship, state and Party ties are good, while the Poles enjoy some domestic autonomy. On the other hand, East Germany and Czechoslovakia are completely subordinate to the Soviet Union, while state and Party relations are also excellent. State and Party ties with North Vietnam are good despite its earlier dependence on China. With China itself, there are good state relations, but disagreements between the ruling parties. Finally, with Albania, there are correct state relations but apparently frigidity in Party relations.

Perhaps the most dramatic illustration of a further change was the reversal of the Soviet attitude toward some organizational expression of unity, like the Comintern or the Cominform. Previously, the Soviet leadership desired such an institution as a means of strengthening its hand. At the conference, Khrushchev is reliably reported to have opposed the very thing he earlier promoted—precisely in order to protect Soviet leadership! In the days when Soviet freedom of initiative was almost unlimited—particularly in the international arena—a Cominform type of organization was useful in ensuring that the other parties followed loyally. The protracted discussions in Moscow made the Soviet leaders sensitive to the possibility that today such an organization could limit their freedom of maneuver. They thus preferred to rely on ad hoc multilateral meetings of Party chiefs, meetings that need not be called regularly and would be less likely to interfere with Soviet international activity.

Furthermore, if Khrushchev's version of the conference can be trusted, it was the Soviet delegation that suggested that the conference no longer refer to the Soviet Party as the leader of the camp. In 1957, the Soviets, supported by the Chinese, had insisted on this designation since the status of leadership helped to ensure automatic support for any Soviet initiatives. But today, as Khrushchev put it, "the fact that we are called the leader gives no advantages either to our Party or to other parties. On the contrary, it only creates difficulties." One may surmise that the elimination of such a reference could forestall any Chinese claim to co-leadership of the camp. In fact, the Soviets might be arguing that if the Chinese want a united, militant bloc, they should respect in practice the Soviet line. Another difficulty that Khrushchev might have had in mind was the danger that the other parties could claim that the formal status of leader puts the CPSU under special responsibility to its followers, and perhaps Soviet freedom of action would be greater without such a formal designation. Finally, the status of leader implied responsibility for actions that the Soviets could not control (e.g., China toward India). In any event, the Kremlin could be certain that parties fully loyal to it would continue to do its bidding. The East Germans, for instance, have continued to make references to Soviet leadership, even though the conference used the vaguer term "vanguard" to describe the role of the CPSU.

This role should not be minimized. As Khrushchev put it in his January address: ". . . the Communist parties must synchronize their watches. When someone's clock is fast or slow, it is regulated so that it shows the correct time. Similarly, it is necessary to check the time of the Communist movement." The emphasis in the statement of the conference on the fundamental importance of the CPSU's experience left no doubt that its clock was to be the "Greenwich Mean Time" of international Communism. Nevertheless, the absence of a formally designated leader, capable of acting as arbiter, is bound to complicate further the international situation in the Communist world, even if abroad it makes the camp look more "democratic." While bringing to bear on any issue its own power, the Soviet leadership must now, to a far greater extent, anticipate the reactions of its followers, especially in view of some of the available options.

The Moscow conference may thus be the end of Khrushchev's search for a new relationship with the bloc. But he did not find what he sought. Indeed, there appears to be a curious and striking parallel between the Eisenhower and Khrushchev records. Both men strove to bolster the power of their countries by making more stable alliances. Yet, in spite of their efforts, or perhaps because of them, they each appear to have presided over a decline in the independent power of their respective nations. Nor did the conference fulfill Chinese hopes. Instead of achieving united militancy, they have contributed to greater heterogeneity within the bloc.

This heterogeneity involves both advantages and liabilities. By appearing less autocratic and more flexible, the Communist camp can now support more effectively the quasi-Marxist regimes in Cuba or Guinea and encourage others in a similar direction. Thus a new type of expansion—indirect—may replace the old, direct type. Many of the new nations throughout the world are not only nationalistic in the nineteenth-century sense; they are ideologically oriented and think in social and economic terms similar to those of Marxists. They use words like "imperialism" and "capitalism" much as the Soviets do. And modernization, which they seek, does not mean to them political democracy. The relationship of the Soviet Union and of the other camp members to these new states is already one of courtship and not Stalin-like domination. In this relationship, the Poles, the Czechs, the East Germans can be of great help to the Communist cause. They civilize Soviet Communism, their social and cultural level makes it more appealing, while the greater internal diversity within the camp makes Communism seem less threatening to the newly independent states.

At the same time, the new external strategy is likely to further the internal processes of change within the camp. One may increasingly expect Soviet allies helping to court a Cuba or a Guinea to seek a "most-favored-nation clause" from the Soviet Union, much the way the East Germans did when the U.S.S.R. was courting Gomulka's Poland in 1956, or the way Latin American states

157

have recently done with the United States, after watching our Marshall Plan aid going to Europe. This is all the more likely because of the new opportunities created for internal maneuvering by the various parties. And these opportunities will probably increase when China acquires a nuclear capability.

From a Western point of view, a prolonged situation of formal Sino-Soviet unity with some degree of divergence is distinctly preferable to an open rupture. A thoroughgoing split would bode ill for the world. The Soviet Union can afford to tolerate within the camp a dissident but lonely China. Thus, a break involving expulsion from the bloc could occur only if China were sufficiently strong to threaten Soviet leadership and to carry with it a significant number of Communist parties. A China capable of unilateral action could be very dangerous. The danger is no less if China should feel strong enough to leave the bloc on its own initiative. Presumably, it would do so only if its leaders felt confident of their ability to go it alone and to influence the course of events more effectively outside the bloc.

In either case, the Chinese would be in control of a significant portion of the international Communist movement. They could thus effectively develop a more actively militant line and presumably back it with their own resources. The Western reaction would necessarily involve a more militant posture also—perhaps the use of force, certainly higher military budgets. Under those circumstances, the Soviet Union would have to follow suit, lest the West gain an over-all military preponderance. Furthermore, the CPSU would inescapably be forced to condemn

Western countermoves to Chinese initiatives, for not to do so would involve an insupportable loss in Soviet revolutionary prestige and probably precipitate further defections to the Chinese side. Hence, a break in the partnership would gradually push the Soviet Union toward more radical attitudes in an effort to regain leadership of the Communist camp. In a world polarized in open hostility between the United States and China, the Soviet Union could not afford therefore to be neutral, and certainly could not side with the United States.

The most advantageous situation from the Western standpoint is one that involves a gradual adjustment of the common Marxist-Leninist ideology to the divergent perspectives of its various subscribers. The existence of the Sino-Soviet dialogue has already forced the Soviet leaders to think through what was formerly only a generalized statement that a war would be disastrous; it has contributed a great deal to increased Soviet sophistication on the subject of nuclear weapons. Unanimity is often a shield for ignorance and, if for no other reason than to argue with Liu Shao-chi, Khrushchev probably had to read some RAND studies! In his emphasis on the destructiveness of a nuclear war, he has come close to admitting that a purely subjective factor, such as someone's decision to start a war, can possibly interfere with an immutable historical process. This necessarily involves a gradual relativization of the formerly absolutist ideology.

Furthermore, divorced from a single power center, this ideology is more and more stretched to embrace the diverse experiences and perspectives of elites, whether on the banks of the Elbe or the Thirty-eighth Parallel.

Increasingly, each party becomes confident that its interpretation of the common doctrine is the correct one.
Ulbricht highlighted this dilemma when he stated in his
account of the Moscow conference that "somebody has
raised the question as to who is the one who determines
what is truth, and what complies with the principles of
the Marxist-Leninist doctrine. There is no easy answer.
Stalin was once the ideological arbiter, and he possessed
the power to enforce his interpretations. Today, the alternative to splits between the parties is some form of
adjustment. Yet, such adjustments mean that the formerly
absolutist ideology is increasingly becoming a relative one.

The Communist leaders are aware that relativization
could lead to dangerous erosion. To counteract it, they are
promoting closer economic ties and integration of the
various members of their camp. In his speech of January 6,
1961, Khrushchev gave special attention to the problem
of unity, insisting that all parties must continuously strive
for it and asserting that the CPSU has made "every effort"
to maintain unity with the Chinese. The Communist
leaders are seeking rapid external victories to keep afire
the sense of an inevitable and worldwide triumph. But
the changes that have taken place within the Communist
world were inherent in its expansion and can be viewed
as part of the process of differentiation that all large-scale
social organizations experience. The West had little to do
directly with the emergence of these changes, and precipi-
tous moves overtly designed to promote splits will only
push the Communist regimes together.

The West can, however, strive to create favorable conditions for the further growth of the diversity that has

160

developed within the Communist camp. We should, for instance, explore the possibility of recognizing Mongolia, thereby encouraging the growth of a sense of independent statehood that almost certainly would lead to more assertive nationalism. We should re-examine critically our policy of nonrecognition of the Oder-Neisse line, since this policy helps to inhibit any Polish regime from "playing the game" of using the Sino-Soviet divergence for the consolidation of its domestic autonomy, and instead forces it to bolster its patron and only source of security, the Soviet Union. We should encourage some of our allies to exploit more the traditional bonds of friendship that have existed between them and some of the nations presently within the Communist camp. We should continue to address ourselves directly to the Communist-controlled peoples, thereby encouraging domestic pressures for change that each regime must now consider, given the greater flexibility of the camp. Finally, we should not make concessions to Khrushchev on such issues as Berlin, in the mistaken hope of bolstering him, but in effect depriving him of the argument he has used against the Chinese—that excessive pressure on the West might lead to a dangerous war. We should consider all these measures, and more.[2] But perhaps it would suffice to note that the Soviet bloc is not immune to the flow of history in the name of which the Communists claim to act. The prophets of history may be gradually becoming its prisoners—and the time has now come for the West to prod history along.

NOTES

Notes

Chapter 1: TOTALITARIANISM AND RATIONALITY

1. Much is made of this in J. L. Talmon, *The Origins of Totalitarian Democracy* (New York: Frederick A. Praeger, 1961).

2. *Totalitarianism* (Cambridge, Mass.: Harvard University Press, 1954), p. 53. The author acknowledges his debt to Carl Friedrich, with whom he has collaborated in teaching a graduate seminar on dictatorship. A product of that collaboration is their book, *Totalitarian Dictatorship and Autocracy* (Cambridge, Mass.: Harvard University Press, 1956; New York: Frederick A. Praeger, paperback edition, 1961).

3. For a fuller discussion, see Brzezinski, *The Permanent Purge—Politics in Soviet Totalitarianism* (Cambridge, Mass.: Harvard University Press, 1956), especially pp. 1-8, 168-75.

4. *Ibid.*, particularly chaps. 4 and 5.

5. Isaac Deutscher, *Russia: What Next?* (New York: Oxford University Press, 1953), p. 227. Deutscher's argument should not be confused with the reasoned analysis of Barrington Moore, Jr., in *Terror and Progress USSR* (Cambridge, Mass.: Harvard University Press, 1954). This weighs alternative patterns of development in terms of the possibility of continued totalitarian development, or a technical-rational pattern, or the emergence of a traditionalist form.

6. For another example, consider the political implications of Kafka's *Trial*.

Chapter 2: PATTERNS OF AUTOCRACY

1. Vladimir N. Kokovtsov, *Out of My Past* (Stanford, Calif.: Stanford University Press, 1935).

2. For excellent descriptions of some of the leading figures in the court life of late nineteenth-century Russia, see the diaries of such dignitaries as A. A. Polovtsev, E. A. Peretz, K. Golovin, and P. A. Valuiev.

3. See, for instance, the texts of the Czarina's letters to the Czar while he was at the front, in F. R. Golder, *Documents of Russian History* (New York and London: The Century Co., 1927).

4. Konstantin Petrovich Pobedonostsev, *Memoires politiques, correspondance officielle et documents inedits relatifs a l'histoire du regne de l'empereur Alexandre III de Russie* (Paris: Payot, 1927).

5. A good source is I. Blinov, *Gubernatory: istoriko-iuridicheskii ocherk* (St. Petersburg, 1905).

6. Marc Raeff, "The Russian Autocracy and Its Officials," in McLean, Malia, and Fischer (eds.), *Russian Thought and Politics* (Cambridge, Mass.: Harvard University Press, 1957), p. 80, mentions the example of a somewhat earlier provincial governor whose routine included signing 270 papers daily, or about 100,000 a year. Recent Soviet discussions of bureaucratic difficulties suggest a striking continuity in this reliance on written and signed instructions: One regional agricultural administration reported that during 1953 it received from the Ministry of Agriculture no less than 7,569 letters; in 1954, 8,459, and an average of about 30 instructions per day (*Partiinaia zhizn*, no. 3 [1956], pp. 60–61). Czarist literature, and more recently even some Soviet, gives us brilliant descriptions of crushed bureaucrats, fearful of inspections, giving their all to the daily dose of instructions, requests, statistics, and so on. See also *Krokodil* for cartoon treatment, and Khrushchev's 1957 speeches on decentralization. For an interesting and informative account of bureaucratic vicissitudes under the Czarist regime, see Flerovsky, *op. cit.*, especially pp. 19–136. He describes his initial career as a civil servant of the Ministry of Justice in St. Petersburg, the internal intrigues and nepotism, the lack of expertise of some of the higher

functionaries, and the rather widespread disregard for established laws and rights on the part of higher and also lower officials.

7. According to the 1879 census, the Gendarme Corps numbered 800 officers and 50,000 men, the police force 104,500 men, and there was an unknown number of Okhrana functionaries and collaborators —this compared to the 435,000 public officials in the same period. (G. Alexinsky, *Modern Russia* [New York: Charles Scribner's Sons, 1913], pp. 178, 182, and 186.)

8. Samuel Kucherov, *Courts, Lawyers, and Trials Under the Last Three Tsars* (New York: Frederick A. Praeger, 1953), pp. 201–3.

9. The Russian criminal code was quite liberal in defining anti-state activities and was even more generous in assigning the death penalty for them. The death penalty was provided for any actions or conspiracies that would endanger the "life, liberty, or health" of the Czar, or would "limit" the powers of the throne (Articles 99 and 101). Furthermore, the death penalty was provided for anyone plotting to change the Russian government, or to change it in any part of Russia, or for anyone plotting to separate any part of Russia from the Russian state (Article 100). The death penalty also was provided for anyone who made an attempt on the life of a member of the Imperial household (Article 105). In addition, "armed resistance to authority or attacks on army or police officials and on all official functionaries in the execution of their assigned duties" were to be punished by the death penalty "if these crimes are accompanied by murder, or attempted murder, infliction of wounds, grievous assault, or arson." See M. I. Gernet, *Smertnaia kazn'* (Moscow, 1913), p. 54. Other offenses, punishable by death, are also enumerated. For various statistics on the frequency of the death penalty, see Kucherov, *op. cit.;* Alexinsky, *op. cit.;* and S. Usherovich, *Smertnie kazi v tsarskoi Rossii* (Kharkov, 1933). These sources also include accounts of mistreatment and flogging of political prisoners.

10. The judges were administratively subordinate to the Minister of Justice. Flerovsky, a civil servant in the ministry, cites cases of the overbearing treatment of the judges by the minister (*op. cit.,* p. 65).

11. A. T. Vassilyev, *The Ochrana* (Philadelphia: J. B. Lippincott Co., 1930), p. 39. See also N. N. Beliavsky, *Politseiskoe pravo* (Petrograd, 1915); and A. I. Elistratov, *Uchebnik russkago administrativnago prava* (Moscow, 1910). Vassilyev, quoted above, was not entirely correct, for, in emergencies, captured revolutionaries were

frequently executed on orders of the provincial governors who based themselves on Articles 17 and 18 of the Special Law for the Preservation of Order.

12. P. L. Lavrov observed in 1870: "Law in Russian eyes never stood on the level of 'written reason,' never became sacred just because it was law. Law was regulation convenient to the momentary whim of the government." ("Philosophy of the History of the Slavs," quoted in J. Kucharzewski, *Od Bialego Caratu do Czerwonego* [Warsaw, 1931], V, 53.) See P. Milyoukov, *Russia and Its Crisis* (Chicago: University of Chicago Press, 1905), especially pp. 165-85, for a general analysis of the weakness of the legal tradition. The failure of the Senate, which was meant to be the watchdog of laws, is illustrative. Filled with retired administrators and even former police functionaries, it never fulfilled its role and became a mouthpiece for the executive. See Flerovsky, *op. cit.,* p. 62, for some specific instances.

13. Merle Fainsod, *Smolensk Under Soviet Rule* (Cambridge, Mass.: Harvard University Press, 1958).

14. Andrei Vishinsky, *Teoriia sudebnykh dokuzatel'stv po sovetskomu pravu* (Moscow, 1941), p. 31.

15. For comparative treatments of the censorship systems, see M. Karpovich, "Historical Background of Soviet Thought Control," in W. Gurian (ed.), *The Soviet Union: A Symposium* (Notre Dame, Ind.: University of Notre Dame Press, 1951); Merle Fainsod, "Censorship in the U.S.S.R.: A Documented Record," *Problems of Communism,* V (March-April, 1956), 12-19; and Alex Inkeles, *Public Opinion in Soviet Russia* (rev. ed.; Cambridge, Mass.: Harvard University Press, 1958).

16. For a detailed treatment of the conspiratorial activity, see A. P. Men'shchikov, *Okhrana i revoliutsiia* (Moscow, 1925–32); and A. Kornilov, *Obshchestvennoe dvizhenie pri Aleksandre II* (Paris, 1905). Count Pahlen reported to Alexander II that the chief reason for the success of revolutionary propaganda was the sympathy that existed for it among large sections of the population (Kornilov, *Obshchestvennoe . . . ,* p. 160).

17. *Pis'ma Pobedonostseva k Aleksandra III* (Moscow, 1925–26), I, 318–19.

18. Cf. Isaiah Berlin, "The Silence in Russian Culture," *Foreign Affairs,* October, 1957, with the following account of a meeting of

young Russian revolutionaries on New Year's Eve, 1880, when arrests were already auguring a not-too-happy future for them:

The preparation of the punch left a particularly plastic image in my memory. On a round table in the middle of the room a vase was placed, filled with pieces of sugar, lemon, roots, sprinkled with arrack and wine. It was a magic sight when the arrack was fired and the candles extinguished. The flickering flame, mounting and waning, lit the severe faces of the men surrounding it; Kolodkevich and Zheliabov stood closest. Morozov took out his stiletto, then another, then another, placed them, crossed, on the vase, and, without preparation, with a sudden impetus, the powerful, solemn melody of the well-known *haidamak* song was heard: *"Hai, ne dyvuites, dobryie ludi, shcho na Ukrainie povstaniie."* The sounds of the song spread and mounted, they were joined by fresh voices, and the shimmering flame flickered, bursting out with a red glow, as if steeling the weapons for struggle and death. [Olga Lubatovich, in *Byloe,* June, 1906, pp. 123–24; quoted in Kucharzewski, *op. cit.,* V, 304–5.]

19. For an interesting recent analysis, see George Fischer, *Russian Liberalism* (Cambridge, Mass.: Harvard University Press, 1957).

20. See Kucherov, *op. cit.;* and Alexinsky, *op. cit.* The latter comments: "To be elected a juror, a man must be a landowner. The composition of the jury was subject to the control of the bureaucracy. . . . Preliminary examinations fell almost exclusively to the charge of the police." (pp. 193 ff.)

21. See S. L. Levitsky, "Legislative Initiative in the Russian Duma," *American Slavic and East European Review,* XV (October, 1956), 315–24; see also S. A. Piontkovskii, *Ocherki istorii SSSR XIX i XX veka* (Moscow, 1935), for a discussion of the electoral system.

Chapter 3: THE NATURE OF THE SOVIET SYSTEM

1. See Barrington Moore, Jr., *Political Power and Social Theory* (Cambridge, Mass.: Harvard University Press, 1958), chap. 2.

2. For a theoretical analysis of this relationship, see William Kornhauser, *The Politics of the Mass Society* (Chicago: The Free Press, 1959).

3. For a discussion of these studies, see A. Etzioni, "Authority Structure and Organizational Effectiveness," *Administrative Science Quarterly*, IV, no. 1 (1959); and the following sources cited therein: Robert Dubin, *Human Relations in Administration* (New York: Prentice-Hall, 1951); M. Dalton, "Conflicts Between Staff and Line Managerial Officers," *American Sociological Review*, L, no. 15; A. W. Gouldner, "Cosmopolitans and Locals: Toward an Analysis of Latent Social Roles," *Administrative Science Quarterly*, no. 2 (1957).

Chapter 4: COMMUNIST IDEOLOGY AND INTERNATIONAL AFFAIRS

1. See Barrington Moore, Jr., *Soviet Politics: The Dilemma of Power* (Cambridge, Mass.: Harvard University Press, 1950), p. 415:

> Students of language have pointed out how the structure of a language may make it difficult to understand, that is, to make the desired responses to concepts that have originated in another language and culture. On these grounds it is at least a reasonable hypothesis that a set of ideas, or a system of political notation, such as Marxism-Leninism, would make certain types of political responses difficult, or perhaps even impossible, whereas it would make others relatively easy. Although the limits of assistance of political notation are probably not as definite as those in the linguistic and mathematical symbol systems, it seems a very probable inference that such limits do exist.

A variant of this problem is raised in Kazimierz Krauz, *Materializm ekonomiczny* (Krakow, 1908). Krauz discusses the inherent proclivity of various social classes to accept or reject certain new social insights without being conscious of the fact that they are, in effect, exercising a selectivity that reflects their interests. He labels this phenomenon "apperception." The emphasis on interest may be misleading, but there can be little doubt that the social conditioning of various groups disposes them to be sympathetic or unsympathetic toward new social insights, or to interpret them in their own manner (but not always in their interest, as Krauz implies), distorting them in the process. A similar phenomenon is discussed in Lucien Goldmann, *Sciences humaines et philosophie* (Paris: Presses universitaires de France, 1952); he calls it *"conscience possible."* For a discussion of both from the Marxist point of view, see Oskar Lange, *Ekonomia Polityczna* (Warsaw: Ksiazka i Wiedza, 1959), pp. 279–82.

2. They also run like a thread through his speeches, recently published in this country: Nikita Khrushchev, *For a Victory in Peaceful Competition with Capitalism* (New York: E. P. Dutton & Co., 1960).

3. It can readily be seen how the combination of Marxism, Western European reformist experience and economic development, and the successes of labor movements within the democratic framework resulted in an altogether different conception of organic and interrelated world change, often spontaneous but still discernible. For the latest Soviet effort to define its world viewpoint, see O. V. Kuusinen, *Osnovy Marksizma-Leninizma* (Moscow: Gospolitizdat, 1959).

4. See the following books for more specific treatment of Communist ideology in Soviet foreign-policy conduct and for evidence of how it has affected that conduct in particular historical situations: Alexander Dallin (ed.), *Soviet Conduct in World Affairs* (New York: Columbia University Press, 1960); R. A. Goldwin (ed.), *Readings in Russian Foreign Policy* (New York: Oxford University Press, 1959; and A. Z. Rubenstein (ed.), *The Foreign Policy of the Soviet Union* (New York: Random House, 1958).

5. For example, Khrushchev's discussion of the reasons why, according to him, Rockefeller's drive for the Presidential nomination met with failure (*Izvestiya*, January 15, 1960).

6. While reading the following citation, the reader might well wonder whether it is not Khrushchev's image of the world:

What is fundamental and new, deciding and permeating all events for this period in the sphere of foreign relations, is that a certain temporary equilibrium of forces has been established between our country, which is building socialism, and the countries of the capitalist world, an equilibrium which has determined the present phase of *"peaceful coexistence"* [italics added] between the land of Soviets and the capitalist lands. That which we at one time thought of as a brief breathing space after the war changed into an entire period of respite. Hence a certain equilibrium of forces and a certain period of "peaceful coexistence" between the world of the bourgeoisie and the world of the proletariat.

At the bottom of all this lies the internal weakness, the weakness and powerlessness of world capitalism on the one hand, and the growth of the revolutionary movement of the workers in general, particularly the growth of forces here, in the land of the Soviets, on the other.

What lies at the basis of this weakness of the capitalist world?

At the basis of this weakness lie those antagonisms which capitalism cannot overcome, within which the entire international situation takes shape—antagonisms which the capitalist countries cannot surmount and which can be overcome only in the course of development of the proletarian revolution.

The statement is not Khrushchev's but is an extract from a 1925 speech by Stalin at the Fourteenth Congress of the CPSU; quoted in Jane Degras (ed.), *Soviet Documents on Foreign Policy*, Vol. II: 1925–32 (London: Oxford University Press, 1952), pp. 69–72.

7. This view is implicit in Professor E. A. Korovin, *Osnovnie Printsipy Vneshnei Politiki SSSR* (Moscow: Pravda, 1951), chapter on "Various Forms of the Struggle of Peace in the Different Stages of Development of the Soviet State," pp. 21–30. For instance, he asserts (on p. 28): "We are for peace also because, armed with the scientific Marxist-Leninist insight and building Communism, we know that time is working for us, that the fall of capitalism as a system is inescapable, and that all roads lead to Communism."

8. M. A. Kaplan and N. de B. Katzenbach, "The Patterns of International Politics and of International Law," *The American Political Science Review*, LIII (1959), 693–712.

9. This leads even some otherwise astute observers to conclude that the Soviet leaders are merely motivated by "the familiar objectives of a great power, to realize its interests and ambitions as one state in a world of rival states." (Louis Halle, in *The New York Times Magazine*, June 28, 1959.)

10. Even today, when the Soviet Union claims to be the world's mightiest power, it justifies the continued need for vigilance and

state power by reference to the existence of systems based on private property. See M. Karpovich in Dallin, *op. cit.;* also Brzezinski, *The Soviet Bloc* (Cambridge, Mass.: Harvard University Press, 1960; New York: Frederick A. Praeger, 1961 [rev. ed., paperback], chaps. 1 and 16, for the application of this Soviet concept of security to practice within the bloc.

11. This view is also implicit in Khrushchev's statement to Adlai Stevenson: "You must understand, Mr. Stevenson, that we live in an epoch when one system is giving way to another. When you established your republican system in the eighteenth century, the English did not like it. Now, too, a process is taking place in which the peoples want to live under a new system of society; and it is necessary that one agree and reconcile oneself with this fact. The process should take place without interference." (Quoted in *The New York Times,* August 28, 1959.)

12. A perceptive treatment of "neutrality of alignment" is to be found in Kaplan and Katzenbach, *op. cit.,* pp. 707-8.

13. Leopold Labedz, "Ideology: The Fourth Stage," *Problems of Communism,* VIII, no. 6 (1959), 1–10.

14. See Moore, *Soviet Politics.*

15. Warnings against this trend have been voiced in the bloc. See, for instance, Romana Granas, "Where is the School of Communism?" *Polityka,* September 26, 1959. This veteran Polish Communist expressed the feeling of many dedicated Communists when she warned that it was easier to maintain a sense of ideological commitment when the Party was out of power. She rejected the excuse that "social consciousness lags behind changes in material reality" as not applicable to Communists who ought to be in the forefront of the struggle and not wait for material plenty to make them into good Communists. An example of the kind of ideological erosion that may take place is provided by *Sovetskaia Latviia,* December 16, 1959, which violently attacks suggestions that were apparently published in Soviet Latvia in 1956 to the effect that the CPSU ought to open its ranks to all able people—i.e., abandon its most elite character.

16. See Brzezinski, *The Soviet Bloc.*

17. It is interesting to note in this connection (regardless of the actual correctness of the assertion) that the importance of purely Chinese factors in the victory of the Communist Party in China is clearly asserted by the Chinese: "The victory of China's revolution

and construction is the result of integrating the universal truth of Marxism-Leninism with the reality of China by the Chinese Communist Party and Comrade Mao Tse-tung." (Teng Hsiao-Ping, in *Jen Min Jih Pao,* October 2, 1959.)

18. L. H. Haimson, *The Russian Marxists and the Origins of Bolshevism* (Cambridge, Mass.: Harvard University Press, 1955).

19. Numerous examples of such apparently varied perspectives can be adduced, not to mention altogether different approaches to India and to Southeast Asian nationalism in general. The following paragraphs from the major statement by Khrushchev in his speech to the Supreme Soviet on October 31, 1959, might well have been addressed to Peking: "We have no reason to fear that the peoples of the socialist countries will be seduced by the capitalist devil and give up socialism. To think differently means not to believe wholly in the strength of socialism, the strength of the working class and its creative abilities." Khrushchev then went on to cite Trotsky as an example of a Communist unable to distinguish between concessions of principle and expediency. On another occasion, Khrushchev warned: "We must make a sensible use of the great advantages of the socialist system and strengthen the world socialist camp in every way. We must not fall behind or go too far ahead. We must, figuratively speaking, synchronize our watches. If the leadership of this or that country becomes conceited, this can only play into the hands of the enemy." (Speech to the Hungarian Party Congress, quoted in *The New York Times,* December 2, 1959.) The foregoing remarks become more meaningful if one considers the remarks that Khrushchev allegedly made to President Sukarno with respect to China, to the effect that the Chinese were pushing their industrialization at "too heavy a cost."

For an official Chinese justification of their domestic methods, refuting all criticisms and incidentally revealing intraparty opposition to such policies, see Liu Shao-chi, "The Victory of Marxism-Leninism in China," in *Jen Min Jih Pao,* October 1, 1959. At one point, Liu Shao-chi states: "To find fault with our big leap and people's communes means to find fault with our Party's general line for building socialism. Who are these people finding fault with the Party's general line? In our own ranks, they are the right opportunists, they represent bourgeois ideology within the Party." He does not reveal who the people outside the Chinese Party are. However, he goes on to assert: "The fact that Marxism-Leninism has lately been disseminated in such a large Eastern country as ours with a population of 650 million and that it has resulted in victory in the mutual practice of the revolution and construction must by all accounts be considered a big event in the history of the development of Marxism-Leninism. Of course, revolution and construction in China have features peculiar to this country. But it is also possible that some of these important special features may reappear in some other country. In this sense, Chinese experience is to a certain extent of international significance." With respect to international affairs, the Chinese seem determined to convince the other Communist parties that the major threat to international peace lies in the warlike intentions of the United States. On the occasion of President Eisenhower's 1960 "State of the Union" message, a *Jen Min Jih Pao* editorial, entitled "What Do the U.S. Presidential Messages Show?" stressed the fact that the purpose of U.S. policy was the promotion of aggression throughout the world. After producing a series of proofs for this proposition and warning against the Western policy of encouraging "evolution" within the Soviet orbit (attacking, incidentally, the report of the Center for International Affairs at Harvard University, prepared by this author, for suggesting such policies), the editorial concluded as follows: "The task of the peace-loving people of the world is to maintain vigilance against all U.S. schemes in the disguise of peace, and expose them, unite and keep up the struggle, defeat the forces of war with U.S. imperialism at their head, and extend the successes of the peace forces of the world." This theme was energetically asserted at the Warsaw Treaty Conference in Moscow by the Chinese observer Kang Sheng, candidate-member of the Politburo. His speech, much more vigorous than the official Conference communiqué, ignored by the Soviet and East European press, was broadcast by the Peking radio on February 5, 1960.

20. A translation of this draft is contained in *Yugoslavia's Way* (Yugoslav Communist Party; New York: All Nations Press, 1958).

21. These views are also concerned with broader international issues, and they frequently deviate from the Soviet version. For instance, recently Erik Molnar, a Hungarian Communist historian, has challenged the standard Soviet position that capitalism is doomed because of the operation of its internal contradictions. The substance of Mr. Molnar's views is contained in a book entitled *Some Economic Problems of Contemporary Capitalism* (Budapest: Szikra,

1959). The theoretical monthly journal of the Hungarian Communist Party, *Tarsadalmi Szemle,* contains a summary of Molnar's views and of the Party's criticisms. According to *The New York Times,* January 10, 1960, the substance of Molnar's views is as follows:

> First, certain social laws that govern the growth and decline of the capitalist system (as defined by the Marxists) can be nullified by the conscious actions and cooperation of the people or the various classes within the framework of a capitalist society.
>
> Second, the laws formulated by Karl Marx about the class struggle and the inevitable pauperization of the people, according to which the exploitation of the working class is inexorably increased, are no longer valid.
>
> Third, the so-called law of general crisis of the capitalist system, as defined by Stalin, cannot be considered valid since World War II.
>
> The role of defense expenditures in a capitalist society does not have the economic and social importance attributed to it by dogmatic Communists. Mr. Molnar advanced as evidence for his position on this point the fact that, though defense expenditures were radically reduced after World War II, unemployment did not increase substantially.

No wonder the new history of the CPSU is designed in large part to provide guidance to the other ruling Communist parties.

22. Speech on December 1, 1959, in Budapest. It is noteworthy that the reactions of the other elites in Eastern Europe, particularly the Poles, but even the Bulgarians, were relatively restrained as far as this particular point is concerned.

23. This led Radek to state: "The attempt to represent the foreign policy of the Soviet Union as a continuation of Czarist policy is ridiculous. Bourgeois writers who do so have not grasped even the purely external manifestations of this policy. . . . Czarism, or any other bourgeois regime in Russia, would necessarily resume the struggle for the conquest of Poland and of the Baltic states, as is doubtless clear to any thoughtful bourgeois politician in those countries. The Soviet Union, on the contrary, is most anxious to establish friendly relations with these countries, considering their

achievement of independence as positive and progressive historical factors." (Karl Radek, "The Basis of Soviet Foreign Policy," *Foreign Affairs,* XII [1934], p. 194.) These words have an ironic meaning today.

24. See Isaac Deutscher, *The Prophet Unarmed* (London and New York: Oxford University Press, 1959). He shows what a gross over-simplification it is to suggest that this was merely a tactical move on the part of Stalin. In reality, this was part of the continuing and often dialectical process of ideology and reality interacting.

25. Moore, *Soviet Politics,* p. 383.

26. Their feeling appears to be based on the following kind of analysis:

The testing of the capitalist system is now historically settled. It is doomed to extinction, to make way for a higher social system—Communism. It is difficult to forecast when this process will be completed on the world scale or the forms it will take. There are weighty grounds for assuming that the Soviet Union's peaceful policy, the growing economic and political power of the socialist camp, and the increasing activity of ever broader masses in the capitalist countries will combine to prevent a third world war. The transition to socialism in some countries may possibly assume comparatively peaceful forms. Marx's idea that the bourgeoisie may be "bought off" in individual countries may become a reality.

The forecast for a briefer period is the following.

In the next ten to fifteen years the U.S.S.R. will draw ahead of the U.S.A. economically and become the country with the world's most powerful economy.

The disintegration of the colonial system will be completed. The former colonies will undergo rapid economic development with help from the Soviet Union and other countries in the socialist camp.

The concentration of capital and rapid technical progress in the advanced capitalist countries will lead to growing unem-ployment and the exacerbation of the class struggle. The desire to prolong the capitalist system's existence will to some extent compel capital to make certain concessions in its contest with the working class.

Cycles will show a tendency to shorten, for with today's

technology the renewal and expansion of basic capital takes place more rapidly than before.

The struggle among the imperialist countries and the antagonistic groupings in the capitalist camp is sure to continue. Apprehension over the fate of capitalism, however, will stand in the way of world wars between these groupings.

The exceptional complexity of the situation involving the historical transition from capitalism to socialism precludes any more specific predictions. [E. Varga, "The Capitalism of the Twentieth Century," *Kommunist,* no. 17, November, 1959.]

27. The November, 1957, declaration of the ruling Communist parties.

28. That the Soviets are already facing this dilemma was illustrated by the following exchange between an Indian newsman and Frol R. Kozlov during the latter's trip to India in February, 1960, as reported by *Pravda* on February 6, 1960:

Question: You have seen our work, our economy and our democracy. Are you convinced in spite of Communist ideology that socialism can be built by peaceful means? Answer [Kozlov]: There is no use in your challenging me to an ideological debate here at the press conference. You know our point of view on this question. We formulated it clearly at the Twentieth Party Congress in full conformity with the Leninist principle of peaceful coexistence of states with different social and political systems. This point of view is that decision in matters of internal development and the methods of the political and economic organization of a society is the internal affair of each nation. The kind of system you have is your affair. We ourselves in the Soviet Union have built socialism and are building Communism, we believe *that under our conditions* [italics added] that is a good way, the only way of development that ensures genuine progress in all spheres of the people's life and an increase in the Soviet people's well being.

While the first part of Kozlov's remarks adds nothing new, the implication of the second part seems to be an acceptance of the proposition that India is building socialism.

29. See H. S. Dinerstein, *War and the Soviet Union: The Revolu-*

tion in Soviet Military and Political Thinking (New York: Frederick
A. Praeger, 1958); and Raymond L. Garthoff, *The Soviet Image of
Future War* (Washington, D.C.: Public Affairs Press, 1959).

30. While formally still asserting the proposition that a nuclear
war would spell the doom of capitalism, Khrushchev's remarks concerning the price the U.S.S.R. would have to pay for such a victory
are bound to have the effect of discouraging anyone from wishing
to pay it: "In various speeches, Khrushchev has said that war
would bring tremendous disaster to all mankind, great devastation
to the U.S.S.R., big losses to the U.S.S.R., and has stated that it
would be a prodigious catastrophe if the United States and the
U.S.S.R. were to fight." (Louis Marengo, "Peaceful Coexistence"
[unpublished study; Cambridge, Mass.: Center for International
Affairs, Harvard University, 1960].) This awareness is accompanied
by a much more sophisticated insight into problems of "deterrence,"
as shown by Khrushchev's discussion on January 15, 1960, of the
importance of a "second-strike" capability to guarantee effective
retribution for a surprise attack.

One may also assume that the Soviet desire to promote an atom-
free zone in Asia in 1958 and 1959 was related to the above considerations and had as its purpose the perpetuation of Soviet nuclear
monopoly within the Soviet camp. These suggestions were studiously
ignored by the Chinese, a consideration not irrelevant to our earlier
discussion. (See Robert W. Barnett, "Quemoy—The Use and Consequence of Nuclear Deterrence" [unpublished study; Cambridge,
Mass.: Center for International Affairs, Harvard University, 1960].)

The Soviet interest in disarmament has also led Khrushchev to
argue in the following somewhat unorthodox way:

> Some people in the West assert that disarmament threatens
> grave consequences for the economy of the capitalist countries.
> They say that if the production of bombs, guns, submarines,
> and other means of destruction were stopped, ruin would
> result and hundreds of thousands of people would be deprived
> of work and a means of livelihood. However, only people who
> see no other way of developing the economy than by sub-
> ordinating it to the interests of preparing for war can reason in
> this way.
>
> The least that can be said about such assertions is that they
> are completely unsubstantiated. I have had occasion to talk with

179

many representatives of American business circles, and the most reasonable of them have nowhere near so gloomy a viewpoint and are confident that U.S. industry is fully able to cope with the task of shifting the entire economy to production of goods for peaceful uses. [*Pravda,* January 15, 1960.]

Chapter 5: THE CHALLENGE OF CHANGE IN THE SOVIET BLOC

1. For instance, O. V. Kuusinen's important work "Foundations of Marxism-Leninism," published early in 1960, and Soviet and Chinese statements on the occasion of Lenin's anniversary in 1960. The Moscow statement itself was apparently prepared originally by the CPSU. This preliminary draft was then reviewed in October by an editorial commission representing twenty-six parties (including all twelve from the bloc) before submission to the conference as a whole.

2. For a fuller discussion of the author's views on policy, see "Political Developments in the Sino-Soviet Bloc," *The Annals of the American Academy of Political and Social Science,* July, 1961; "Moscow's Real Goal," *The New Leader,* August 14-21, 1961; and, with W. E. Griffith, "Peaceful Engagement in Eastern Europe," *Foreign Affairs,* July, 1961.

DATE DUE